Blockchain Masterclass for Businesses and Corporations

SHAKRUDDIN KHAN

Published by SHAKRUDDIN KHAN, 2023.

Also by SHAKRUDDIN KHAN

The Smart Way To Personal Finance Success
Goal Setting 101 Achieve More Goals Than Ever! Faster!
Blockchain Masterclass for Businesses and Corporations

Table of Contents

Copyright

Blockchain Masterclass for Businesses and Corporations

Book Design by **SHAKRUDDIN KHAN**

About

Are you looking for a quick, highly-effective and easy way to understand blockchain and Bitcoin, without wasting countless hours sifting through unnecessary filler information?

Do you want to get a firm grasp on what blockchain and Bitcoin are all about? Even topics such as Smart Contracts and Digital Tokens?

Do you need to quickly learn the key concepts and vocabulary around blockchain and Bitcoin?

This effective guide will help you understand blockchain and Bitcoin, including more advanced topics such as smart contracts and digital tokens, and will set you well on your way to blockchain and Bitcoin mastery.

This Book will help you quickly master the most important ideas and topics in blockchain and Bitcoin.

I look forward to seeing you inside!

How Big Is Bitcoin?

So how big is Bitcoin really now in this chapter of the Book, we're talking more about the market cap, the size of the asset class of cryptocurrency and bitcoin, more than the technological revolution that Bitcoin really is. So this is looking at where we are on the adoption curve. How big is this asset class in comparison to some of the other major asset classes we have around the world? And when we do this, let's first not take my word for it.

Let's take a look at some of the smartest, most educated billionaires around the world. So Elon Musk says cryptocurrency bypasses current controls. Paper money is going away and crypto is a far better way to transfer value than a piece of paper, that's for sure. Paul Tudor Jones, one of the most famous billionaire hedge fund investors in the world, says the best profit maximizing strategy is to own the fastest horse. If I'm forced to forecast, my bet will be Bitcoin. Shamos Polycarp Attia owns Social Capital, one of the, you know, one of the most forward thinking billionaire investors in the world and also a very early investor in Bitcoin says it's Money 2.0. It's a huge, huge, huge deal.

Also, the CEO and founder of Twitter, Jack Dorsey, as well as CEO and founder of Square and Kashef, says the world will ultimately have a single currency. The Internet will have a single currency. I personally believe it will be Bitcoin. So these are some of the smartest people on Earth. And usually when you're looking for good advice, you follow the money, you follow where the money is going. You look at what they do and not what they say. Now, these are all billionaires that are coming out in favor of Bitcoin.

And this year in 2020 alone, we've seen a flood of institutional money starting to flow into this asset class as really a hedge against the world government, the world monetary system that we just explained in the last chapter. But these are some of the smartest people on Earth. These are some of the most well-educated, well versed people on earth. And they're all putting their faith and their dollars into Bitcoin. But where are we on the adoption curve? How big is Bitcoin and really how far will it go? How much can we expect it to grow? And so for this, let's take a look back in time.

This is the logarithmic growth curve of Bitcoin's price over time. And so, as you see, we started early in 2010 here at just over about 60 cents. And then we go to where we are today in late 2020 at over twenty two thousand dollars. Now we can see this growth curve follows a pretty standard exponential growth path. And as we look at this logarithmic growth curve, what we need to realize is that this is not a standard graph. This goes from one cent to 10 cents to a dollar, ten dollars, one hundred thousand, ten thousand and one hundred thousand. Now, what we can see is that if we expect the ending of this market cycle to touch this kind of upper band where it's touched in the previous cycles, we can expect a Bitcoin of roughly 100000, maybe even higher than one hundred thousand by the end of twenty twenty two.

This seems like astronomical growth, but if we look back in history, we can see that this emerging new asset class has had this type of exponential growth pattern. But one of the major criticisms of Bitcoin in the past has been, whoa, it's just it's way too volatile. I don't want to invest in it because, you know, we see these thousand percent moves to the upside and then we see 80 percent or 90 percent corrections and then these massive dips and valleys and peaks. And it's just way too volatile. So it must not be a good asset to invest in. And what I'd like to say is that volatility is a symptom, that the market size, it's not a symptom of market weakness. And so if we think about a market that's only one hundred million dollars large, in order to make that market double, you would only need one hundred million dollars of added value to make that market double.

In contrast, for a market the size of gold, 10 trillion dollars in order to make gold double in price, you would need an additional 10. A trillion dollars flows into that market, so as market size continues to grow, volatility tends to level off because you need more inflows or more outflows at a certain time in order to make that price move. So let's take a look back and let's imagine the Internet had a price. You could buy stocks or you could buy shares on the Internet when it was first invented. Let's call it the 1970s. Well, if you bought that stock, you would see the same amount of volatility as you're seeing. And because as you saw in the fledgling kind of early creation stages of Bitcoin, not the massive peak and valley of the dotcom boom and bust, this would be an extremely volatile asset as well. And the fact of the matter is that price discovery is always a volatile process.

When there's a revolutionary new asset or new technology in play, price discovery will be volatile. But as that market size continues to grow, volatility tends to level off. And so even in the past year, we've seen volatility in Bitcoin almost cut in half. We're seeing declines instead of the 30 percent pullbacks we saw in the last bull market in twenty seventeen. This year we've seen our first pullback and it was only 17 percent. So volatility is decreasing over time. And as this market continues to grow, I expect that volatility to continue to decrease. But the fact of the matter is that we are still so early in the Bitcoin development process and on our path to mass adoption. Let's take a look at a different metric.

This is what's called the stock to flow model. And this was introduced by someone on Twitter that goes by the pseudonym of Plan B. And what this graph represents is a visual representation of Bitcoin's price as it relates to the event. And if you remember from our previous chapter talking about mining, Bitcoin goes through a holding event every four years where the Bitcoin mining reward gets cut in half every four years. And what this effectively does is it cuts out the amount of outflow into the market by half. And so when outflows get cut in half and then the demand either stays the same or gets increased, the price tends to increase in an exponential fashion. Now, if we take a look at this color graph, we can see that when the color is purple, it means we're very close to the next tabbing.

And then once it turns red, we had just had our having. So in the past, we've had three stabbings in the past. What we see is an exponential price move right after this. Having as the market takes into account the reduced outflow into the market, we see this massive exponential price move, a settling off and kind of a leveling until the next having excuse me, until the next having where we get another exponential price move and then a leveling off and until the next having. So this is where we are today. We just are having an in May of last of this year and we are pushing forward to our next exponential growth period. And then we will level off essentially until the next housing and then we'll push forward for more exponential growth.

Now, this stock to flow model is not necessarily perfect. There have been criticisms in the past of the way this model is developed. But as of today, it is the best. It is one of the best metrics that we have. And it has actually followed this price curve pretty much to the T.. And what we're seeing is, as we expected after having, we're seeing a boom in price. So what we can expect is this market cycle will likely take us to roughly the end of 2022. And if we see an overshoot in price like we've seen in the past, past market cycles, we could see a price peaking out in the 150 to 200000 range before dipping back below the fair value line and leveling off here until the next day. So from a twenty thousand dollar price range in just over a year and Half or two years, we could see a five to 10x move in price. This is absolutely unheard of in other asset classes.

I mean, a market of scale like this is a once in a generation investment opportunity. And we've seen that in the past. We've seen tens of thousands of percent moves to the upside. And as I said in the very first chapter of this Book, one of the very first chapters Bitcoin over the past decade has grown over nine point two million percent. This is unheard of for many asset classes and has truly been the highest performing asset of all time. So we're seeing this trend continue. We're seeing this growth into the stock to flow model. And hopefully by the year, kind of the end of twenty two here, we'll see a leveling off of the price, maybe a dip below fair value and then another another having. So this stock to flow model is a great representation that you can use to see if Bitcoin is over undervalued. There is a link here and the documents. So feel free to go to the site, look into bitcoin dotcom. There's a lot of great charts on there, including the logarithmic graph from the previous chapter.

OK, now let's take a look at not only the price growth that we expect over the future, but just how big this market is in comparison to some of these other classes around the world. And what we see is that right now we are here. We are so, so small in comparison to some of these larger asset classes, like like corporate stocks, like gold currencies, and even just the richest people on Earth like cryptocurrency is it pales in comparison to even, you know, the wealth that's accumulated by the billionaires in the world. So we have a long, long way to go now. Let's take a look first at the global stock market.

The global stock market is 70 trillion dollars, maybe even higher than that at a time of recording. And first, before I go any further, I just want to explain, for those who don't know what market cap actually is, market cap is the size of an asset or the size of an asset class. And what that is, is the price of the asset times, the circulating supply. So in the case of a stock, how many stocks are in circulation times? The price of the stock, that is, gives you the market cap. And right now, the market cap for Bitcoin is roughly about four hundred and forty billion dollars. So less than half a trillion dollars. And the market cap for all global cryptocurrency. So everything that's being built on this block change space is only six hundred and eighty billion. So still less than a trillion dollars.

This is a market that's still in its infancy, well over a decade in, but still so, so small in terms of its relation to the global stock market or the global bond market, which even makes the global stock market look like petty change. And so we can see we still have so much room to grow, even in terms of the size of some of the biggest companies we have on Earth. If we look at Bitcoin, which could potentially be a global reserve as a global currency, it's still smaller than some of the biggest businesses we have. So this really shows you where we are in today's adoption curve and how much room we still have to grow. If we take a look in the same way at the richest people on Earth, we have a net worth of eight trillion dollars in the hands of just over two thousand people.

Eight trillion dollars. That's 44 percent of the world's wealth, owned by the richest one percent. This is, you know, a wealth disparity that is not sustainable. And the reason it's gotten so big is because of the current market dynamics that I explained in the last chapter. When new liquidity and new government printing of money goes into circulation, it starts in the hands of large corporations. And the first people to touch that new printing usually reap the most benefit from it. So these billionaire business owners are really reaping the most rewards from the new liquidity that's coming into the market. And this is why we've seen such a growth in wealth disparity over time.

So this needs to be done. And Bitcoin is potentially something that can allow that to change.

It's one of the first assets that we've ever had where the regular everyday person can front run some of the biggest companies can front run some of the biggest investment firms in the world. And you can purchase it yourself. You can own this asset and let it grow over time like a savings account would. If you purchase this asset. There's only a scarce amount. And as these billionaires and investors want to get in, they have to buy it from the same currency supply that or from the same monetary supply that you have. And so the earlier you get in, the higher the price goes as these new institutional asset classes or institutional investors start to come into the space. Now, let's take a look at the gold market . We've done a lot of comparing gold and bitcoin, but as we said in the last chapter, Bitcoin is really gold 2.0. So even for it to get to the same market size as gold today, which is 10 trillion dollars or maybe even higher by this point, with all the with all the printing that's going on just to get to the market cap of gold, the price of one single Bitcoin would need to get to about five hundred thousand dollars.

Half a million dollars per bitcoin, and we're currently at a price of just over 22000. This is truly remarkable. And to think that not only is Bitcoin similar to gold, but it is a better substitute for gold. It's more transferable, it's more transactional. It's easier to send online over large distances. And so it has all these qualities of gold, as we talked about. But it's Gold 2.0. It's better. So what if this even surpasses the market cap of gold? This is what we really have to look forward to in the future of

Bitcoin. And then finally, let's take a look not just at gold, but at the current currency supply in the world.

And the M1 currency supply, which is physical cash in circulation, is about five trillion dollars. But the broad money supply, which includes cash and credit and liquid liquid currency, essentially is over 80 trillion dollars. So I'm not saying this is going to happen anytime soon, but I'm saying let's take a look at the bullish perspective. What if Bitcoin gets to a place where governments are holding it, where institutions are holding it as a reserve asset, where it truly becomes a global reserve? What could we expect in price?

Well, if Bitcoin was to replace the broad money supply, one Bitcoin would be worth three point eight million dollars. Now, I'm not saying this is going to happen overnight, and I'm not saying this is going to happen right away, but it does look very likely that we are moving in that direction. We're starting to see large corporations reduce their cash reserves and put those cash reserves into Bitcoin. We haven't seen the first government yet, but I assume in the next few years when hyperinflation starts to ravage some of these Third World countries, we are going to see national reserves start to buy up Bitcoin as a hedge on their current monetary system.

This is the stage that we're in today, and this is how exciting it is for those who own Bitcoin to see what the future might hold, to see how this asset class might grow over time, and how that might affect yours and your family's wealth. As we start to see some of this, some of this wealth changes hands in the greatest wealth transfer in human history. So thanks for thanks for watching that. I look forward to seeing you in the next chapter as we talk about our path to this mass adoption.

Billionaires on Bitcoin

When you do your research on any topic, you usually want to learn from the best. A good principle to follow when it comes to investing is to "follow the money." There is a reason Billionaires become Billionaires... They tend to spot trends and make sound investments before the average person. With that said, let's take a look at what some of the top Billionaires say about Bitcoin: Elon Musk: "Cryptocurrency bypasses current controls... paper money is going away. And crypto is a far better way to transfer value than a piece of paper, that's for sure." Paul Tudor Jones:

"The best profit-maximizing strategy is to own the fastest horse... If I am forced to forecast, my bet is Bitcoin." Chamath Palihapitiya: "It's money 2.0... it's a huge huge huge deal." Jack Dorsey: "The world ultimately will have a single currency, the internet will have a single currency. I personally believe it will be Bitcoin." Stan Druckenmiller: "Frankly, if the gold bet works the bitcoin bet will probably work better because it's thinner, more illiquid and has a lot more beta to it,"

This is just a shortlist of some of the biggest names and their comments, however, over the Book of 2020, we saw a flood of institutional investors coming out publicly in support of Bitcoin.

Logarithmic Price Growth

People are very good at understanding linear growth, however, we are not as capable of understanding exponential growth and the effects of compounding. This way of thinking comes from an evolutionary bias. When we age, we age one year at a time. If we hunt, we have enough food for the next day. Nature tends to evolve in a slow and predictable fashion. There are not many instances in nature where exponential curves occur.

The price of Bitcoin is an area where linear growth does not apply, and instead, we must learn to think exponentially. Bitcoin's price has grown exponentially over time, and there are no signs that it has plans to slow down any time soon. The chart below shows the price of Bitcoin on a logarithmic scale (meaning the scale grows by an order of magnitude as it goes up).

Bitcoin Volatility We can see that although the asset has been volatile in the past, its growth consistently represents an exponential curve. But why is Bitcoin so volatile? The fact of the matter is that the volatility of Bitcoin is a symptom of its size, not its weakness. Understanding this is easy. For an asset 10 trillion dollar asset like gold to double in price, you would need an additional 10 trillion dollars to flood into that market.

However, for an asset like Bitcoin (at only 500 billion) to double in size, it only needs about 500 billion to flow into the market. Emerging assets are more volatile because they have smaller market caps. Imagine Investing In The Internet in 1969

Imagine you could invest in the internet as a technology in the early days of its creation. Imagine how volatile the price of the internet would be. It would have seen some parabolic runs, as well as major busts (after the Dot com bubble for example). Bitcoin is the same way. It is experiencing its period of volatility, but will eventually stabilize as it continues to grow.

Why does Bitcoin grow Exponentially? Bitcoin is the first time we have combined money with a social network. To understand why Bitcoin grows exponentially, we need to understand Metcalf's law of network effects. Metcalfe's law states "the effect of a network is proportional to the square of the number of connected users of the system (n2). Therefore, as more people adopt Bitcoin, the price grows in an exponential fashion.

Stock-to-Flow Model

The Stock-to-Flow Model was popularized by an Anonymous writer on the internet named Plan B. The model is used to predict the price based on the Bitcoin currency supply, and the algorithmic reduction in new supply minted (halvings). The more scarce the asset, the higher the price will go, therefore halvings in new supply have a tremendous effect on price. Over Bitcoin's history, it has followed the model almost to a tee.

The model shows that the reduction of currency supply every four years tends to lead to exponential price moves to the upside. The model predicts that by the end of 2021, we may see a Bitcoin price of roughly $100,000, and by 2026 the price might be upwards of $1,000,000! These types of price predictions can seem absurd to some, however, it is important that we keep in mind the exponential growth of Bitcoin as a result of Metcalfe's Law, as well as the macro-economic factors that are forcing the adoption of Bitcoin around the world.

Cryptocurrency Market Cap Comparisons

It is easy to look at the recent run of Bitcoin and think the asset looks overvalued, but when we compare the size of Bitcoin to some of the other asset classes around the world, we realize that we haven't even scratched the surface of its future potential. The chapters below give a visual representation of the size of the cryptomarket in comparison to other major global assets around the world. By comparing the size of this asset class to others, we can see how small cryptocurrency still is relative to more established markets.

Taking a step back to look at these comparisons is important to get an understanding of how much room this market still has to grow. Cryptocurrencies are currently a market of scale and as Bitcoin continues to rise in price, it creates a tide that raises all ships in the cryptocurrency space. Market Capitalization = Price x Circulating Supply Bitcoin Market Cap: $500 Billion (at time of writing) The market cap of Bitcoin is a drop in the bucket compared to some of the larger asset classes in the world. As Bitcoin reaches mass adoption, there is nothing stopping it from reaching or surpassing some of these massive valuations. Entire Cryptocurrency Market Cap: $740 Billion The entire cryptocurrency industry (outside of Bitcoin) is currently only valued at 240 Billion.

The companies that are building the next generation of applications and software are currently extremely undervalued in comparison to their predecessors. Global Stock Market: $70

Trillion Bitcoin is currently on 0.7% the size of the global stock market Bitcoin is currently less than 1/4 the size of Apple Billionaire Net Worth: $8 Trillion There are currently roughly 2,900 Billionaires in the world The wealthiest 1% of the world owns more than 44% of global wealth (This is not sustainable in the long term) Gold Market Cap: $10 Trillion If Bitcoin Meets Gold's Market Cap, One Bitcoin Would Be Worth roughly $500,000 per Bitcoin As we learned in chapter 20, Bitcoin outperforms gold on almost every single property of money. There is a high potential that Bitcoin will not only reach the market cap of gold but surpass it due to its programmability and ease of use.

M1 Money Supply: $5 Trillion The M1 money supply is the total amount of physical money around the world. It does not include digital money that is lent out by the bank in the form of checking and savings accounts. Broad Money Supply: $80 Trillion Add in checking accounts, savings accounts, money-market accounts. Not quite physical money, but you can still make a bank transaction digitally and use that as money. This is called broad money,[1] and according to the CIA World Factbook[2], the global total is in excess of $80 Trillion. If Bitcoin became more of a transactional currency and replaced the broad money supply, it could hypothetically get to around $3.8 Million per Bitcoin.

"Most of the broad money in the world economy isn't actually cash held in bank vaults," explains Karen Petrou, Managing

1. https://www.investopedia.com/terms/b/broad-money.asp

2. https://www.cia.gov/library/publications/the-world-factbook/rankorder/
   2215rank.html

Partner at Federal Financial Analytics. "It's bank balances on digital ledgers, money that people deposited in banks, and banks then lent out again."

The Path to Mass Adoption

OK, so now we've taken a look at the history of money and we've taken a look at the history of Bitcoin and kind of how it's gotten to where it is today. But the next stage of this is seeing how we get to that mass adoption, how we get from a global population where a fraction of a percent of people own cryptocurrency to the majority of people starting to use and transact with cryptocurrency on a daily basis.

Now, as we dive into this, we can learn that every new technology or every innovation goes through an adoption curve. And so this adoption curve goes something like this. In the first kind of chapter, we have the innovators. These are the pioneers, the people that wait in line to get the new iPhone as it comes out, the ones that hold the torch for the next kind of phase of the population to start adopting this new technology. Then you get into the early adopters, a slightly larger percentage of the population, but still the people that are ahead of the curve that want to be early, that want to, you know, kind of front run the technological advancement, then you have the early and late majority.

This is when the majority of the population starts to come in. And then you have the laggards, the people that, you know, still have dial up phones that will do anything and everything not to change their ways and to continue using legacy technology. These are the laggards. They come in last. And as this adoption curve continues to go, we see this diffusion of innovation. So this is the percentage of the population that adopts the technology. And this is the kind of distribution that we see and how it gets adopted. So we are about here with crypto currencies. We're still in the innovators stage. Less than a percent of the population has crypto. And we're still very much in the pioneering phase.

It's mostly owned by either large institutions, people that want to front-run what they think is going to happen in macroeconomics and those pioneers that have been here since day one. The Bitcoin ogg's that are really continuing to drive this market now in order to get to mass adoption, you need to really get buy-in from three major groups. You need to get buy-in from governments. So in terms of policies and regulation, you need to get buy-in from corporations. So their innovation in their investment and you need to get buy-in from people. They're the ones using it. They're the ones investing in it. They need to know, you need to essentially get people to buy into a technology in order for it to be adopted. So we are still so early on this curve. And for all those people that think it's too late to get into Bitcoin, the long arc of history hasn't even seen a fraction of what Bitcoin can do and how Bitcoin will revolutionize the world.

And so it's it's you need to sometimes take that macro step out, that ten thousand foot view to see where you are in the adoption curve of Bitcoin, even though we've seen this price run up so much in the past ten years. OK, let's take a look at these. Each individual group. The three groups that need to get to mass adoption. Let's look at people. How do we know that people are adopting Bitcoin? Well, there are a few different metrics that you can look at. You can look at the transaction value. How much money is being transacted on the network. You look, you can look at the transaction count, so how many transactions are actually happening and the beauty with all of this is that it's open source. So all of these transactions are transparent and easily viewable on the block chain. But the one most important metric that I think is crucial to understand the true adoption of Bitcoin is the hash rate.

This is how much computing power is going into securing the network, or in other words, how many computers are mining the Bitcoin algorithm, as we talked about in that kind of mining chapter. Now, this is what we've seen in Bitcoins history. This is the mining hash rate. And over time we've only seen this hash rate continue to grow. What this tells me is that, yes, there's still economic benefit to mine and people are willing to use their energy to mine this Bitcoin. So the people believe in it, the miners believe in it, and therefore the community tends to believe in it. So the more hash rate or the more hash power there is on a network, the more miners that that means, the more secure the network is.

So the more secure the network is, the easier it is for more people to adopt, the easier it is for institutions to adopt and the easier it is for governments to create regulatory policies that will allow for the next stage of innovation. So this is a very important metric. I've put a link in the PDF to coin metrics . This is where I pull this information from. But you can also take a look at many different other metrics, transaction count and value as only one of them or few of them. But it has a ton of great information, not only on Bitcoin but on other cryptocurrency as well. So I highly recommend if you're interested in doing your own research, take a look at coin metrics.

OK, well, how do we get to corporate adoption and what are some metrics that we can look at to see if corporates are really adopting this and what we're seeing today in 2020, which is a step change different than any of the other cycles that we've had in the past, is that corporations are truly adopting Bitcoin as a new reserve asset, not only as a speculative investment to try and increase their dollar returns, but they're using it as a store of value. Instead of having a bunch of US dollars on their balance sheet, they would prefer to have Bitcoin on their balance sheet because it holds its value more than the dollars that are getting printed into existence. So we're seeing massive companies like MicroStrategy put four hundred and fifty million dollars of their cash reserves into Bitcoin.

And additionally, in the last few weeks, we've seen MicroStrategy take out another debt financing round of six hundred and fifty million to put it into Bitcoin as well. We've seen Square put one percent of their cash reserves into Bitcoin, 50 million dollars. And from that we've seen an institutional flood. You can see all these different corporate entities that own Bitcoin. And I've also left a link to Bitcoin Treasuries, dawg. So Bitcoin Treasuries, dawg, will allow you to see in real time the balance, the balance sheets of Bitcoin owned by all these corporations. And as those corporations continue to get more and more numerous, we're going to see this kind of ledger continue to grow with all these new corporations starting to adopt the technology. So right now, we can see clearly that there's population adoption from the mining community, the hash rate, transaction count, etc. We can see there's corporate adoption because they're looking at Bitcoin as a reserve asset. And on top of that, not just corporate, but some of the safest, you know, institutions on Earth, some of the institutions that have the lowest risk profile.

Take the insurance company, MassMutual, for example, they just invested one hundred million dollars into Bitcoin. These institutions have an extremely low risk profile because they don't want to invest their money into anything that's going to fall in value over time because then they would go insolvent if they had a bunch of insurance claims. So even the companies that have extremely low profiles of risk are looking at Bitcoin as a hedge, as a store of value and as this new global monetary system. OK, the last stage of mass adoption to get to mass adoption, we need governments to adopt the block chain.

We need governments to adopt block change in order for Bitcoin to become part of that, you know, everyday use case where you can transact it with Canadian dollars or U.S. dollars and use it as a store of value in an exchange around the world. Well, what are we seeing happen right now as a result of covid-19? We've seen mass printing to a level that we've never seen in history and in the same way that the global governments needed to have a Bretton Woods moment in 1944, we're seeing those same governments look together and say we need a new Bretton Woods moment. Now, that Bretton Woods moment, I suspect, is going to be a mass move to central bank digital currencies. What this means is that we're seeing a lot of the major countries around the world building, developing and piloting these central bank digital currencies that are their own currencies in themselves, but built on top of the block chain, built on top of this fundamentally secure transaction layer.

And as we see the adoption of central bank digital currencies, this makes it easier for the adoption of Bitcoin and other cryptocurrency because they can transact with these central bank currencies that are built on the block chain. It makes it a lot easier for this new financial system to transact with a legacy financial system. And even though these central bank digital currencies will not have the same fundamental qualities that Bitcoin has in terms of scarcity and dispersion and decentralization and being directly peer to peer, there will still be a government in the middle.

They will act as a great bridge to help people get from that legacy financial system into this new financial system we call cryptocurrency and block chain. So this is a graph of the status of central bank digital currency development across countries around the world. And we see almost every major country around the world, either in active working groups or interested or piloting their own central bank digital currencies. I think within five years we're going to see central bank digital currencies adopted on a wide scale around the world with all the major economies starting to move to digital currencies, to this digital currency state.

And once that happens, we are going to see an inflow of capital to block chain based currency systems that we've never seen in history. And once that liquidity moves into block chain based currencies or central bank digital currencies, it makes it easier for them to move into Bitcoin. So this is a wealth transfer to the level that we have never seen in human history. It hasn't even been recorded in human history for us to look back on. And this is a movement that's happening on a global scale right now. These global G7 and and G20 countries are looking, looking at each other saying, whoa, we are printing way too much money.

This is not sustainable. We need to move to a new system. That new system is blocking. That new system is central bank digital currencies. And as I said over and over, that adoption will become easier and easier as we get more and more countries building these central bank digital currencies. So the path to adoption is a lot closer than we think. And with this inflow, this avalanche, the tsunami of institutional money and government investment in block chain, I think this bell curve, this diffusion of innovation will come a lot faster than many people think. Thanks for reading. I look forward to seeing you in the next chapter. Cheers.

Getting to Mass Adoption

It is great to look at the market cap comparisons in the last chapter and dream of what Bitcoin could eventually become. But it is another thing entirely to plot out how we will actually get there. The good news is that Bitcoin is making inroads in all the necessary facets of society in order for it to get to mass adoption. Every new innovation goes through an adoption curve, this is called the Diffusion of Innovation.

The categories of adoption may sound familiar:

Innovators (0% - 2.5%): The pioneers of new technology. The one's building, testing, and writing about new products and advances in technology. These are the trailblazers. The ones willing to stand in line for days for the newest iPhone, or the latest pair of Air Jordans.

Early Adopters (3% - 13.5%): These are the people that purchase the newest gadgets, and that always seem to have the latest update or the latest version of hardware or software technology.

Early/Late Majority (: This is where the bulk of the population lives. These people see the trend and realize they need to make a change. Late adopters may need some prodding from their friends, but eventually, they fall in line.

Laggards: Older generations tend to be laggards of technology adoption. They are content with what they have and would rather be the "same-old" as opposed to learning something new.

It is important to note that as we look at the Diffusion of Innovation chart, we are still very much in the "Innovator" phase. In fact, only 1.3% of the world's population currently owns Bitcoin. There is a long way to go to get to mass adoption, so we must remember, this is a market of scale, and holding these assets now will set you and your family up for success 10, 20, 30 years into the future.

How To Achieve Mass Adoption In order to reach mass adoption of any technology, you need to have buy-in (or at least consent) from three major constituents. People - There needs to be a use case, and investment from the general population Corporations - You need to have companies building products on top of the technology Governments - You need to have policy makers and regulators allow for the technology to grow sustainably and responsibly. It can generally be said that if you win over two of these constituents, the third will follow suit, either intentionally or out of necessity. Let's look at some metrics we can use to assess adoption from these three major constituents.

Consumer Adoption

Bitcoin is one of the first technologies that were able to reach user adoption before most corporations even knew what it was. There are many different metrics you can cite for user adoption, but one of the most telling stats is the Bitcoin Hash Rate.

Hash Rate is the measuring unit of the processing power of the Bitcoin network. The greater the hash rate, the more computing power there is mining Bitcoin.

This is a great indicator of network adoption because these miners are using large amounts of electricity to power the network. The more people mining the Bitcoin algorithm, the more secure the network. This not only shows that the security of the Bitcoin network continues to increase, but also that miners are willing to outlay capital to pay for the electricity... This equates to people willing to buy a good or service. We expect Hash Rate to continue to increase as the price of Bitcoin increases.

Corporate Adoption

The path to corporate adoption was dramatically accelerated in 2020 due to the COVID virus and the response by world governments. As governments continue to print trillions of dollars in response to the virus, companies are looking for alternative reserve assets to store their wealth. In the past, most companies would hold some portion of their treasury in USD.

However, with the currency being debased, and the value of the dollar depreciating, corporations are looking for a new reserve asset that will not only store their value but also provide some amount of yield over time. Corporations are not looking to trade Bitcoin. They are not looking at it as a way to make returns on their investment, they are simply looking for a safe haven that can shelter their wealth and that won't depreciate over time. Corporate adoption can become a virtuous cycle.

No one wants to risk their reputation being the first person to invest their treasury in Bitcoin, but no one wants to be the last either. Once the first corporation does, then the risks are greatly diminished. As new companies start to purchase Bitcoin, more companies follow. Sooner or later companies start to have fear of missing out, and they all pile in at once.

We are still early in this process, but the first few dominos have already fallen... MicroStrategy: Invested 445 Million into Bitcoin (55% of cash reserves) - Later purchased another 650 Million in Bitcoin through debt financing Square: invested $50 Million (1% of cash reserves) - They also published an open-source patient on the entire process, making it easier for other companies to follow suit.

Galaxy Digital Holdings: Invested $134 Million (now represents 74% of their market cap) Mass Mutual: Invested $100 Million in Bitcoin - The first large scale insurance provider to take a stake in Bitcoin Grayscale Bitcoin Trust: Currently owns over $15 Billion in Bitcoin - they are the largest corporate holder of Bitcoin There are many other big name companies that now hold a significant portion of their balance sheet in Bitcoin. This is only the tip of the iceberg. If you would like see more corporations that have invested in Bitcoin visit the link below:

BitcoinTresuries.org: https://bitcointreasuries.org/

Government Adoption

In October, the Managing Director of the IMF announced the need for a "New Bretton Woods moment[1]." It has become clear that this statement made reference to the global adoption of Central Bank Digital Currencies.

Central bank digital currency is the digital form of fiat money. The present concept of CBDCs was directly inspired by Bitcoin, but CBDC is different from virtual currency and cryptocurrency, which are not issued by the state and lack the legal tender status declared by the government.

At present, most major countries around the world are either piloting or developing a CBDC strategy. CBDC's will give the government unparalleled control over the supply and distribution of currency in their country. They will also most likely serve as a great on-ramp for many to get into the cryptocurrency space.

Crypto On-ramp One of the major barriers to entry into the cryptocurrency space is the legacy financial system. Our current monetary system was not built on the blockchain, so it is still difficult to switch back and forth between fiat and cryptocurrency. Once governments adopt programmable money, in the form of CBDCs, the on and off-ramps for crypto will become even more seamless.

---

1. https://www.imf.org/en/News/Articles/2020/10/15/sp101520-a-new-bretton-woods-moment

How to Buy and Store Cryptocurrency

OK, now let's get into the part of the Book I know most of you are waiting for how to buy and store your cryptocurrency. Now, there are many different ways to do this based on risk tolerance, based on your objectives, be it short term or long term, and also based on the amount of value you'd like to invest. So I'll go over a few different options for you. If you are new to the cryptocurrency space and you just want to whet your toes a little bit, I would recommend starting with Coinbase.

Coinbase is North America's largest crypto exchange. They are a great place to start because they have a very simple UX, UI and application. It's a smooth process to send your funds via credit card and they have a pretty wide selection of crypto currencies that you can choose from. Those crypto currencies on the exchange have all been vetted and approved by Coinbase, so they are more reputable than just any old coin you hear about on the street. That being said, they do have pretty high fees, three point nine nine percent fees, in fact. So those can definitely eat into your savings over time. Now, if you want to explore the wonderful world of alt coins, I would recommend finance.

Finance is the world's largest cryptocurrency exchange. They're based in China and have listed hundreds of different cryptocurrency. They have fairly low trading trading fees, just about 75 basis points per trade. So if you do want to explore that world of coins, finance is a great place to do so. Now, if you are an institutional investor or if you were a high net worth individual, ultra high net worth individual, or if you run a corporation or institution that you would like to get involved in Bitcoin or cryptocurrency, I highly recommend that street. That street is Canada's Canada's fastest growing digital asset exchange. We currently have over 100 million in trading volume and over 50 million in assets under management.

We have the lowest fees in the industry and also the largest liquidity for any cryptocurrency in the space. Now, that said, we do work specifically with high net worth individuals and the minimum trade value is twenty five thousand dollars. So if you fit that category, that street is definitely the place to go. And you can also reach out to me if you would like to start trading with that street and I can help you get up, get set up yourself.

Finally, if you're somebody that would like traditional rails and just doesn't feel comfortable diving headfirst into the crypto space, you can also use some traditional investment tools to get exposure to Bitcoin. Now, I've listed two different options here, one for Canadians and one for Americans. Now Greyscale and Kubicki or three IQ is the company. These are Bitcoin trusts. Now they purchase Bitcoin. And when you buy shares in their company, you get exposure to the underlying asset. Now, you don't own the Bitcoin, but you own the exposure to the assets. So it's a great place to get exposure to the price movements in Bitcoin.

You can invest in these assets through your TFSA or your IRA and they can be very tax advantaged in that respect. The ticker symbols for both our BTC, for Greyscale and Kuis BTC for three IQ. Now, how to store your cryptocurrency. There are also a few different ways for this, depending on your preference. Now let's start with exchange. Custardy exchanges are many of the things I just listed. Finance and Coinbase are exchanges. There's also hundreds of other exchanges, too many to list. But just know that crypto exchanges are a great place to purchase cryptocurrency, not necessarily a great place to store your cryptocurrency. So these places can get you access to crypto. But I would highly recommend not storing a large amount of value on these exchanges.

The reason being is because they are all connected to the Internet. And when you have your funds connected to the Internet, there is always a possibility that they can be hacked. So the best practice is to take your funds and to store them in cold storage, either with a custodial service or with your own self custody. And I will talk about that in a second. So a great, great way to do that is through centralized custody. Now, I've listed a few custody options here, but there are many that you can choose from Coinbase Custody, Bingo and Fidelity Digital Assets are three of my favorites. And actually that Street has a partnership with Coinbase Custardy. So if you would like to store large values with them, you can absolutely do that through State Street as well as the pros to the side are these companies are offering security as a service. So you don't need to worry about your private keys.

You don't need to worry about making sure your funds are safe. These companies will do it for you. They funds in cold storage and they make sure they are doing all the due diligence to ensure your funds are safe. Now, the downside to this solution is that you have to pay for it. Security as a service means you have to pay. These fees are usually very small, but over time they can tend to eat into some portion of your savings. That's just something to keep in mind. But if you don't want to, if you don't want the hassle and the responsibility of managing and owning your own keys, you can absolutely trust a custodial service like one of the ones listed here.

OK, if you'd like to earn interest for your Bitcoin or your digital asset, you can use a service like Block PHY. I believe these companies actually allow you to stake your digital assets and earn interest on them. When you loan or lock up your coins with these companies, they lend them out to institutions, to hedge funds so they can invest them and earn a return on the funds invested. So this is a great way to put some of your cryptocurrency to work. I wouldn't recommend putting your entire savings in these types of financial options, but it is a great way to put a little portion of your savings to work and actually earn up to an eight percent or 10 percent interest on some of your coins.

Moving right along this, I believe, is the safest way to store your cryptocurrency, but it also is the highest responsibility for you and it is self custody. Now, there are a few different hardware wallets that you can purchase, but two that I would recommend that are the biggest brand names in the industry are Tresser and Ledger. Now, you buy these hardware wallets and you offload all of your crypto from exchanges onto these hardware wallets so they're not connected to the Internet. Now, the benefit of these devices is that your funds cannot be hacked or stolen unless somebody actually steals your physical hardware wallet. So if you do invest in these hardware wallets, I would highly recommend you keep them very safe and you keep copies of your private key and your recovery phrase in separate places to ensure there is not a central point of failure for somebody to hack and steal your funds.

Now, this is definitely the safest way to store your funds because you always have physical access to your funds. However, there is definitely an added level of responsibility. So with great power comes great responsibility and you need to understand the risks of having self custody, one of them being that you lose your keys, you lose the recovery phrase or the keys that allow you to access your funds. This can be extremely worrisome for people, and that is why many people tend to opt for centralized custody so that they don't have to worry about that. The other risk with self custody is duress. So if somebody understands that you're heavily involved in crypto and God forbid they come and hold a gun to your head, that could be one way that they could steal all your funds all at once. So you need to be very, very careful with where you are storing your hardware wallets and how you're keeping your recovery phrase and your private keys safe.

Now, another thing that I would recommend is if you're going the self custody route to be very, very secure with your assets. So it's not enough just to have them on a hardware wallet. You need to make sure that that hardware wallet is safe so you can get a safe for your house. You can store it in a safety deposit box at the bank, but ensure that not only the hardware wallet, but also the recovery freeze and the private keys are in a safe place. And never, never, never send your private keys or send your recovery phrase to anyone online. If you ever see a website or a company asking for either of those things, it is most likely it is definitely a phishing attack attempt or a hacker. So please never enter either of those things online.

Now, a golden rule is to make sure that the security of your assets is equal to, you know, the value of your assets. You're not going to, you know, spend a thousand dollars on a big safe in a hardware wallet. If you've only got, you know, fifty dollars or a hundred dollars in crypto, it just wouldn't make sense in the same way. It wouldn't make sense if you have millions of dollars in crypto and you leave it on a centralized exchange. So ensure that you are treating.

This, like your money, you need to make sure that you have security that equals the value of your assets, and I will leave it to you to distinguish what that might be. So anyways, that is a good explanation on how you can purchase and how you can store your cryptocurrency. I hope you enjoyed it. And I will see you in the next chapter. Cheers.

Where to Buy Cryptocurrency

There are many different ways to purchase cryptocurrency, and each avenue has its benefits and disadvantages, depending on your technical savvy and your risk tolerance. I have listed a few easy ways to buy cryptocurrency, depending on your preference. Coinbase: [1]Coinbase is the largest cryptocurrency exchange in North America. It has an extremely easy-to-use interface and your account can be funded directly from your credit card. While the experience is clean and easy, you certainly pay for it.

Coinbase takes a 4% fee on all deposits as well as a 0.5% spread on all trades within the platform. If you are new to cryptocurrency and just want an easy way to get some exposure, this may be a good option for you. Review Coinbase Trading Fees[2] Binance: [3]If you would like exposure to the broader altcoin market, one of the best exchanges to do so is Binance. Binance is the largest crypto exchange in the world. They are a Chinese company but have headquarters in the US as well. Their trading fees are very low (0.075%) and they have hundreds of altcoins listed on the platform. It is easy-to-use and free to transfer currency in and out of your account.

Review Binance Trading Fees[4] Satstreet[5]: Satstreet is a high-touch cryptocurrency brokerage working exclusively with

---

1. https://www.coinbase.com/join/granti_p

2. https://help.coinbase.com/en/coinbase/trading-and-funding/pricing-and-fees/fees

3. https://www.binance.com/en/register?ref=12766698

4. https://www.binance.com/en/fee/schedule

high-net-worth individuals and institutions to help them get exposure to Bitcoin and other digital assets. They have a $25K transaction minimum which allows them to source deep institutional liquidity and very competitive rates (roughly 1% all-inclusive). However, they are currently only operational in Canada. Grayscale[6] / 3iQ[7]: If the entire world of crypto still scares you, and you would prefer to get exposure through traditional financial instruments like your TFSA, RRSP, or your IRA, you can turn to Grayscale Bitcoin Trust or 3iQ Bitcoin Trust.

These companies are publicly traded under the ticker symbol (GBTC) and (QBTC) respectively. Grayscale is an American company, while 3iQ is Canadian. The success of these fund's mirrors that of Bitcoin because their value is derived solely from Bitcoin. One thing to note is that buying these funds does not actually give you access to the underlying asset, Bitcoin. You cannot withdraw Bitcoin from Grayscale and spend it yourself. You are merely getting exposure to the price movements. You pay a slight premium on the price of Bitcoin, but some investors will find this worthwhile so they can stay within the financial instruments they are comfortable with.

---

5. https://satstreet.com/?ref=bitcoin-101

6. https://grayscale.co/

7. https://3iq.ca/

How to Store Your Cryptocurrency

Just like there are many ways to purchase cryptocurrency, there are also many ways to store your cryptocurrency. Each method has its pros and cons depending on your risk tolerance and the value of your assets. Exchange Custody: While exchanges are a great place to buy and sell a cryptocurrency, it is highly recommended that you do not store large quantities of money on an exchange.

Most exchanges in the crypto space are still centralized entities, and therefore they are susceptible to attack. One of the most infamous exchange hacks ever came from Mtgox.com where over $1 Billion worth of Bitcoin was stolen from the exchange.

Centralized Custody: Centralized Custody solutions tend to be preferable for institutional investors, as there is a company responsible for safeguarding your funds. Most of these solutions require multiple signature authentication, meaning at least two signing authorities need to be present in order for you to access the funds.

Centralized Custody adds an extra layer of security, as well as peace of mind that you do not need to manage your own keys. There is a fee associated with this solution however, most companies will charge 0.5% -1% per year.

Centralized Finance: Now you can make your crypto work for you. If you transfer your Bitcoin onto lending platforms like BlockFi, they will pay you up to 8% annual interest on the Bitcoin you deposit. Interest is paid out daily and you can withdraw your funds at any time.

BlockFi is also ensured so you can rest easy that your crypto funds are secured. If you are planning to buy and hold long-term, solutions like BlockFi may be a great way to earn interest on your funds. However, one of the downsides of this type of custody is that it will trigger a taxable event when funds are withdrawn from your lending account.

Self-Custody: One of the most secure ways to hold your funds is through self-custody, although there is a huge level of the added responsibility that comes with this. If you chose to store your funds on a hardware wallet, you are responsible for your own funds. If you lose your password or your back-up phrase, you may lose your funds. You also need to ensure that your hardware wallet is stored somewhere safe. It may be a good idea to invest in a safe, or a safety deposit box to ensure your wallet is safe.

A General Rule: Ensure the amount you invest in security makes sense relative to the value of your assets. If you only have $100 in crypto, you probably don't need to buy a $150 hardware wallet to secure your funds. On the other hand, if you have millions invested in crypto, you should ensure that you are investing in solutions that will provide you peace of mind and safety for your assets.

Crypto Taxation

Each country will have different policies when it comes to the taxation of your crypto assets, so I did my best to pull information on how crypto will be taxed in North America. Links to these websites can be found in the resources: Canada: How cryptocurrency is taxed in Canada The Canada Revenue Agency (CRA) has issued guidance that Canadian taxpayers are liable for taxes on crypto. Furthermore, crypto is not considered to be a legal tender currency; rather, it is treated as a commodity.

Cryptocurrency is taxed in Canada as either capital gains or as income tax, depending on whether your activity with cryptocurrency is considered to be a business or not. 100% of business income is taxable, whereas only 50% of capital gains are taxable at your respective tax bracket. If you're unsure whether you are operating on a personal or a business level, consult with a tax professional. What crypto transactions are taxable in Canada?

The CRA states that a disposition of cryptocurrency results in taxable consequences. These dispositions, or taxable events, are as follows: Selling crypto for fiat, i.e. CAD Trading crypto for crypto Using crypto to buy goods or services Making a sale or gift of crypto Resource:

https://www.canada.ca/en/revenue-agency/programs/about-canada-revenue-agency-cra/compliance/digital-currency/cryptocurrency-guide.html

United States: In the US, crypto is treated as a capital asset, and any sale of crypto is subject to capital gains tax. When you sell crypto, you calculate your capital gain or loss based on the difference between the sale price of the crypto and its adjusted basis. What's the adjusted basis? Well first, the cost basis is how much you paid for your crypto. The adjusted basis is the cost basis minus expenses like transaction fees and commissions.

With regards to the cost basis, the IRS has not given any explicit guidance on how to identify cost basis in crypto sales or exchanges (since you can sell a bunch of crypto at one price but acquire units of it at different prices).

Resource: https://www.irs.gov/businesses/small-businesses-self-employed/virtual-currencies

Australia: Tax treatment for cryptocurrencies under the Australian tax code is similar to the US tax code for the most part. Under the Australian tax code, cryptocurrencies are treated as a "form of asset" and subject to capital gains taxes. Therefore, selling, trading, or exchanging cryptocurrency and converting it into Australian dollars or a foreign currency or using it to obtain goods or services can trigger taxable events. Record keeping is also essential similar to the US tax system.

Resource: https://www.ato.gov.au/General/Gen/Tax-treatment-of-crypto-currencies-in-Australia—-specifically-bitcoin/[1]

---

1. https://www.ato.gov.au/General/Gen/Tax-treatment-of-crypto-currencies-in-Australia---specifically-bitcoin/

The Future of Blockchain

OK, let's move into the final chapter of this Book, what might a block chain based future look like? Now, this is a big question and nobody really knows the answer, but it's important to dig into how we think people's perceptions might change of what is true and what can be trusted. Now, let's first dig into the current social contracts that we have. I think people are going to start to move more from brand based contracts to math based contracts. And what does that mean?

You know, we have put in some of the biggest brand names on Earth here, right? Visa to Apple and some of the biggest banks and insurance companies in the world. Right now, we trust that these companies will act as good actors because there is competition in the market. If this steals your money, you might switch to MasterCard. So they have an incentive to be good actors and to to essentially act and act in a positive way as good citizens kind of in the community. And the reason we've always had trust in these big brands is because they've earned our trust over the years and over the past as we say, kind of over 100 years or just under one hundred years.

We haven't really had a true financial meltdown that would force these big companies to become bad actors, to become insolvent or not to be able to service their debts or service their requirements to their customers. So we've always just kind of thought, you know what, we trust these companies because they've been around so long and because they have the brand behind them. That is a brand based contract. Competition and game theory prevents bad actors and we trust them to assess counterparty risk and to essentially give us the benefit of the doubt and to to be to be good actors.

Now, what we're going to see is a shift to math based contracts to people no longer just trusting in the brand because it's a good brand. People will start to focus on algorithms that will eliminate the possibility of bad actors as opposed to reputation that eliminates the bad actors in these systems. There is no trust needed. You no longer need to trust these brands to act in good faith. You just trust the algorithm that it runs as it should. This removes all counterparty risk. So you no longer need these companies to assess counterparty risk. This will eliminate it in total and it will also allow for settlements to happen in seconds, not weeks, because they're not on the block chain as opposed to third parties. And it will allow for the elimination of billions of dollars in banking fees.

The way all of these banks have gotten rich is by taking a percentage of every one of your transactions. So moving from this concept, from this paradigm as a society of, OK, we have trust in this brand because it's a brand to move to. We have trust in math. We have trust in this algorithm because the way it's coded allows it to work. That is a big shift and that is a big paradigm shift that we will see as a result of blocking. We're also going to see mass disruption across almost every single industry in the world, similar to the Internet, how the Internet started to eat up every single industry and those who didn't adapt to an Internet based business were left in the dust.

We're going to see the same thing happen with the block chain. So that's going to happen in banking and payments. That's going to happen in the insurance industry where things need to be insured and provable and trusted on the block chain. You're going to see this in health care. You're going to see identities on the block chain and you're going to see health care records be tied to each individual patient kind of in a secure and safe cryptographic way. You're going to see real estate start to become tokenized on the block chain. People can become fractional owners of a house or fractional owners of a certain land development instead of having to own the entire asset. And so then you can get exposure to these increasing asset values without needing the entire capital to buy the entire thing.

This will revolutionize land ownership for a lot of the emerging world ridesharing programs. Imagine an Uber that was decentralized and instead of Uber taking 20 percent of all the driver fees, drivers get to keep 100 percent of all the fees that they earn. So if you drive out, you drive for a couple of hours on a decentralized Uber platform, the application and the user experience might look exactly the same, except you get to keep all the money you make instead of paying your tax to Uber.

Same thing's going to happen with supply managed supply chain management. The block chain will revolutionize the amount of information we have about where a product is and how it gets to each place in the supply chain with provable timestamps on the block chain. We can see when a project, when a product or. Service gets from one stage to another and the route that it takes to get to the final user networks and

Iot are going to be completely disrupted because people are going to be able to transact value peer to peer authentication. So driver's license and government identity, cloud storage and decentralized cloud storage, you no longer have to rely on Google or Amazon for their centralized computing power. You can rely on computing power that's in computers all over the world. And any additional computing power or computer storage that your computer might have, you can add to the block chain and in turn get paid for it by people who need the space.

The music industry is going to get revolutionized, artists are going to have more ownership over their work, over their art streams are going to be able to be paid and micro payments by companies back to the artists. So the artist is going to have more ownership over their work in their passion. The retail industry is going to change. You're going to be able to start spending and paying. And Krypto gambling is also going to change, especially online gambling, where you can have block chain based casinos where the outcomes are provably fair based on hashes on the block. Chain prediction markets also are going to be revolutionized. For example, A.I. based prediction will allow, you know, to a high degree of certainty people to predict what outcome might happen in the future and then also for people to bet on those predictions.

And then energy management will also be revolutionized, very similar to the way that supply chain management is revolutionized by the block chain. Energy management will make it easier for energy sources to get to the people who need it with less kind of centralized energy production. So there will also be newer industries that will emerge kind of as revolutionary new spaces based on block chain and the development of this ecosystem, one of them being decentralized finance. And we're already seeing this develop today in the same way that we talked about Block VI as a centralized finance solution.

Decentralized applications are already being built and used today. In fact, there's over 15 billion dollars already locked up in decentralized finance applications. And what that means is all this all this company or corporation is is a smart contract. That, you know, you input your funds into it, lock up the funds and the funds get borrowed and lent to anybody who needs them, and you were in all of the interest from the funds that you're supplying. So all of the value goes back to the end users, back to the suppliers, as opposed to being siphoned off by a centralized company.

We're going to see decentralized governments. We're going to see businesses that, for example, one like Cardno that's building governance systems into the block chain. So provable voting and ways to choose the outcome of what might happen based on block chain based secure trust, less voting. We're going to see tokenized natural resources so people will have an incentive to, for example, sustain the wildlife in Africa or to conserve the rainforest based on tokenized natural resources. You're going to see decentralized insurance. So in the same way we have decentralized finance, you're going to have smart contracts that have in their code to pay out if a certain function happens. So, for example, if a farmer takes out insurance that if it doesn't rain a certain amount of times in a given calendar year, their insurance policy pays out. There's no claim. There's no need for, you know, conversation with an insurance company and a struggle to try and get your money back.

It's unequivocal. If X happens, Y gets paid out, decentralized insurance will change the industry. Micropayment, as I talked about, for example, for content creators, creators or artists, instead of getting paid by Google for every time an ad shows up on your on your video, you would get paid specifically for the likes on this decentralized platform or for the comments or for the amount of engagement that you have on your video. You it gets rid of the need for advertising based models and moves more towards quality content, making quality money decentralized, i.e., this is a space that I'm extremely interested in because I believe that if we're going to have a benevolent A.I. in the future, it needs to be decentralized. We can't trust the development of A.I. as it is today.

Right now, the hands of true AI development are in the hands of a few hands. Facebook, Amazon, Google really run the growth of A.I. and, you know, essentially governments and whatnot. And right now, the way that we're teaching A.I. is extremely scary right now. Right now, A.I. is used in the military to kill. It's used in retail to attract buyers for people to buy. It's used by governments to spy on people, facial recognition and tracking. And, you know, in these ways, we're bringing up this kind of almost emerging life form. This baby, we're teaching it to kill, to spy, to steal and to gamble. With prediction markets.

And we're teaching these kids to use for fear, kind of almost corrupt gambling. And so this is not the future we want to see for A.I., a decentralized A.I. has a much higher chance of being benevolent and actually being good for society because the power is distributed by the people who use it and it's built by everyone who needs it. So it's built kind of with the end community in mind as opposed to the goals of the corporation in mind. This is an extremely powerful technology and we need to make sure that we're being good stewards of it. We're going to see fractional ownership, like I talked about in real estate. We're going to supply chain based identities, which is going to be huge for the developing world. And those are some major revolutions that we're going to see and innovation now for all coins to watch.

Now, one of them is already up there, but we'll start with a theorem. A theorem is a global decentralized supercomputer. So essentially what that means, it's an open source platform for building new applications, for building new smart contracts. On top of that you can think about it like the operating system of iOS or Linux. How? Or Windows. Where you have Windows, the operating system that runs on your PC, but you can also build applications on top of that that allow it to run more, more smoothly. So think about Ethereum as a platform where people can build new applications on top of all built on the block chain, chain link and polka dot. First, let's talk about chain links.

Chain link is an Oracle solution. So chain link is a way for smart contract protocols, mostly based on a theory, but built on other protocols as well to get real world data and pull it into the block chain. So currently block chains are very good at, you know, understanding the truth of what happens within them. But they're very poor at bringing in real world data that happens outside of the block chain. And how do you prove that that real world data is true if it's being pulled in from another third party source? Well, chain link solves that chain link helps bring kind of real world either weather data or, you know, sports data. Stock market data pulls it into the block chain so different smart contracts can be executed based on the information that it's getting pulled in from the real world. So this explodes the use cases of block chains.

It allows block chains to be used for trust, less transactions for trust, less communication between the real world and the block chain based world. Polka dot is another great protocol that I'm excited for. Polka is a third generation block chain, Bitcoin being a first generation, Ethereum being a second generation. Pochoda is a third generation and it is a meta protocol, almost a living protocol that allows you to build smart contracts on top of build block chains on top of. But also it has an underlying governance system and agency to be able to update the protocol in a way that works for everybody. So this is an extremely exciting step forward in the kind of protocol space to allow us to not only build these smart contracts, but to have an underlying almost organism that is growing and building on top of this, you know, to make the entire system work better, smoother and faster.

And finally, singularity is a personal favorite of mine. This company is building a decentralized A.I., like we just talked about, the importance of decentralized, decentralized A.I. But this is a marketplace for different eyes to actually communicate with each other. If you built a a narrow A.I. that was very good at seeing and somebody else built a narrow A.I. that was very good at hearing and another person around the world built a narrow A.I. that was very good at image recognition, all of these eyes could communicate and could be kind of packaged up together into a robot that could not only see but hear and and recognize images. As this ecosystem in this marketplace continues to grow.

We're going to start to see the emergence of a general intelligence or a general A.I. that can do things similar to how humans do, but tenfold better, faster and stronger. And so this is a really important project, not only for the development of the block chain space, but also for the development of the human race. And I think it can't be understated how scary Proposition eight is. But how much a space like this needs to be ported into the block chain, into a distributed, decentralized fashion that allows the development to be kind of in the best interest of all parties involved.

Now, as I keep saying, over the next five years, we are going to see the biggest wealth transfer in human history and the law of conservation of wealth means that people who are people who have wealth will do everything that they can to conserve it. And so in order to make sure that you were on the right side of history, if you educate yourself on these changes that are taking place and on this new technology that's emerging and burgeoning in this industry, you can be on the right side of that wealth transfer. You can make sure that you get in early enough to reap the rewards, to reap the benefits of these exponential technologies and the exponential gains that will come from them. And finally, in the end, markets will always choose what is bigger, faster and stronger. This is a general characteristic that makes the mechanism of markets so incredibly powerful.

And in the end, it is my guess and my money. I'm putting my money on crypto. So thank you so much for watching this Book, for consuming all of this information. I know it is a lot, but this is the first step to you starting to build your own arsenal of information and starting to build on your own knowledge of this new technology. And I hope you continue on this path. I hope you get down a rabbit hole and you learn all the great things that crypto has to offer. I hope you share this with your friends and family. And thank you again so much for watching. So much for supporting the Book shares. And we'll see you in the next one.

Mass Disruption

Just like we saw with the internet, we will see massive disruption in almost every industry and institution we know. Businesses will need to adapt to blockchain or die.

Banking & Payments - The role of the banking sector will get taken over by Central Banks as Central Bank Digital Currencies go live. Alternative decentralized finance platforms will become mainstream and lock-up trillions of dollars in lending pools.

Insurance - The insurance industry will become decentralized and will be executed by smart contracts on top of the blockchain. Claim disputes will be a thing of the past as blockchains will source provable and verifiable evidence that claims should be paid out.

Healthcare - Healthcare records will be stored on the blockchain and owned by the individual. People will have the right to choose which companies get access to their medical records and will be able to get paid for sharing their data.

Real Estate - Real Estate will become tokenized and ownership will be recorded on the blockchain. Fractional ownership will become possible, allowing people to own fractions of Real Estate all around the world. Developing countries will be able to distribute the cost of real estate, allowing the rate of construction to increase.

Ride-Sharing - Ride-sharing platforms will become decentralized. Car owners will be able to accept trips and get paid for their service without paying a 20% fee to Uber or Lyft. Supply Chain Management - Supply chain management will become traceable and verifiable on the blockchain. The flow of goods and materials will be recorded on the blockchain to ensure authenticity and/or fair trade.

Networking & IoT - Machines will become connected and will pay each other for the services they provide. Your car may end up paying for toll roads itself. Authentication - Identities will be stored on the blockchain. You will be able to verify your identity through a barcode on your phone. Cloud Storage - Cloud storage will become decentralized. Services like Apple iCloud & Amazon AWS will compete with cheaper, more secure decentralized computing power. Your computer will be able to connect to these decentralized shared storage centers and earn you money by providing idle storage space to the network.

Music Ownership - Artists will record songs on the blockchain and automatically be paid micro-royalties every time the song is played or used. Retail - True brand name products will be embedded with blockchain-based bar codes to prove authenticity. Gambling - Blockchain authenticated trust will become the norm in online casinos. Random hashes will determine the winning roulette spin or the winning slot and provably fair online gambling will become commonplace.

Prediction Markets - Data oracles will aggregate prediction markets from around the world to determine accurate odds and payouts for prediction markets and spot betting. Energy Management - Energy grids will use blockchain-based payment systems to evenly distribute power amongst a community. You will be able to store solar energy and sell it back to the grid for a profit. Devices will become smarter and more energy-efficient reducing energy waste and ensuring even distribution.

Brand Based vs Math-Based Contracts

We trust large insurance companies because they have a game-theory incentive to act in good faith, or else their customers would switch brands. However, when insolvency becomes a forefront issue due to currency debasement and poor currency distribution, we will learn to stop relying on companies solely based on their brand name. Math based contracts are far more reliable, secure, and beneficial for the end consumer.

Math based contracts have no incentive to overcharge for their services. They do not need to create a financial return for their shareholders, and therefore they can afford to operate at a much cheaper cost to the end consumer. Math-based contracts remove all counterparty risk. Insolvency is not an issue because a 1:1 ratio of funds are held in escrow until certain criteria are met. If the criteria are met, the payment can be paid out algorithmically within seconds... no claims, no disputes, no hassle.

New Industries Emerge

It is impossible to comprehend all the new industries that will emerge from the blockchain. Just as it was impossible to predict what new industries would arise from the internet. With that said, here are a few new industries that are already emerging in the blockchain space.

Decentralized Finance - Decentralized Finance (Defi) is disrupting banks and financial institutions. We are already seeing a flurry of businesses building financial technology that interoperates and stacks together like lego blocks. There are already billions of dollars locked up in decentralized finance applications that allow you to earn yield, take out loans, and borrow against collateral. The difference is, these applications can earn you 8-10% interest on your Bitcoin...

You'll have a hard time finding another savings account in the traditional financial world that pays anywhere close to that. Decentralized Government - Modern-day governments are big, slow, and ineffective. We need a new way to make decisions, settle disagreements, vote, and fund public works as a society. Blockchain-based companies like Cardono are already building decentralized governance systems that will eventually be able to run nation-states.

Voting can be as easy as opening an app on your phone (how this isn't already a thing in 2020 is beyond me...). Cardano is also building decentralized funding mechanisms. Portions of the network fees. Tokenized Natural Resources - We will never be able to save the planet so long as a tree is worth more chopped down than growing tall, or a whale worth more dead than alive. Our incentive systems for environmental sustainability are fundamentally flawed. Tokenization of natural resources allows for people to invest in the conservation of nature. Imagine you could invest in tokenized chapters of the rainforest and therefore own a portion of all revenues from new medicines developed in that land. There would be an inherent incentive to conserve the land and diversity in order to optimize for financial gain in the future. Imagine buying "air-futures" and your investment paid out if a certain percentage of pollution reduction was met within five years. These concepts can apply to ocean conservation, and endangered species as well.

Decentralized Insurance - We spoke about this in the last chapter, but less follow-up with an example. Imagine a farmer in Africa was able to buy crop insurance that paid out if there was not enough rain in his village one season. Oracles will provide real-world data to smart contracts that can pay these policies out instantly if certain criteria are not met. Micropayments - Micropayments will open up a world of opportunity for decentralized social media networks and content creators. Imagine a platform that paid out fractions of a cent for every view, like, comment, or repost of your content. This is possible and already being developed on the blockchain.

Decentralized AI - AI is one of the most exciting as well as scary concepts of the future. However, a world where AI is owned by centralized companies does not look promising. Large corporations and governments are currently incubating the next generation of AI. Currently, its main use case is to Kill (military), Sell (corporations), Spy (governments), and Steal (gambling). This is not what we should be teaching the artificial general intelligence of tomorrow. Blockchain and distributed AI is the best way to increase the likelihood of a benevolent AI. If the AI cannot get harnessed and co-opted by centralized actors, it stands a chance of serving the best interest of the people.

Companies like Singularity Net are already working on this. Fractional Ownership - One of the safest assets to own is real estate, however, many people cannot afford a house by themselves. With fractionalized ownership, you can have the ability to purchase fractions of real estate, or fine art, and reap the benefits of their accruing value over time. Blockchain-Based Identity - Blockchain-based identity may be the most important feature of the blockchain for the developing world. There are currently billions of people around the world who do not have access to government-issued identification or documentation.

Currently, the economic system is leaving these people behind. Blockchain-based identity will allow those who need it most, access to the financial system, and in turn, upward economic mobility.

The World of Alt-Coins

The cryptocurrency space is far more than just Bitcoin. Although Bitcoin will most likely be the reserve asset of the future, the entire space is teeming with a Cambrian explosion of new businesses that will challenge the Goliaths of today. These companies/assets are commonly referred to as "alt-coins". While there are too many incredible alt-coin projects to name, I have created a list of some of my favorite projects in the alt-coin space.

Ethereum - Ethereum is a global decentralized supercomputer. Its native currency ETH, is used to pay for computing power on the network. If Bitcoin can be thought of as "digital gold," ETH can be thought of as "digital-oil". Ethereum is an open-source platform with a complete coding language used to build decentralized applications & smart contracts. This may very well be the operating system of the future.

Chain Link - Without real-world data, blockchains aren't very useful. They are very good at proving what happens within the blockchain, but not great at understanding what happens outside of them. Chain Link solves that. Chain Link is an oracle solution, it pulls real-world data into the blockchain so it can be used to execute smart contracts. This will be incredibly important as more and more applications start to build on top of the blockchain.

Polkadot / Cardano - These are both separate protocols, but I lumped them together because their goals are similar. Bitcoin is a first-generation cryptocurrency. Ethereum is a second-generation cryptocurrency. Polkadot and Cardano are both third-generation cryptocurrencies. They were both built by ex-co-founders of Ethereum (Gavin Wood & Charles Hoskinson respectively). Their goal is to solve the "scalability trilemma" that Ethereum has struggled to solve. They want to build a protocol that is scalable, secure, and sustainable.

These protocols also have built-in governance systems that allow their communities to vote on how they grow and adapt. Singularity Net - This is personally one of my favorite projects in the crypto space. They are working towards building a global, decentralized marketplace for AI's that will eventually become a decentralized artificial general intelligence.

AI's within the marketplace will be able to pay each other for their services and autonomously create organizations to accomplish a given task. Their founder and chief scientist is Ben Goertzel, one of the world's leading minds in AI and creator of the Sophia robot. This project is still years away from commercial use, but if they accomplish what they set out to do, it could be the greatest technological achievement in human history. All of these coins can be purchased on Finance.

The Biggest Wealth Transfer In Human History

With this, we draw our Book content to a close. But before we do, I wanted to finish with a few thoughts. Conservation of Wealth Wealth is a lot like energy, it is never destroyed, it is merely transferred from one form to another. We are currently witnessing the biggest wealth transfer in human history. If you educate yourself on this technology, you too will be on the right side of that history.

Conservation of Power: A Future with decentralized technology is not a given... Those in power will do whatever they can to retain power. Regulators will try to stifle innovation and keep centralized power as long as they can. This outcome will enrich the few, and enslave the many. We must fight for decentralization with our voices and our wallets.

Market Theory Markets are a beautiful thing. At the end of the day, the market will decide who wins and who loses... But the market is the people, and the people are the market. People always choose what is better, faster, stronger... in the long run, my money is on crypto.

Closing Thank you so much for supporting the Book and for sticking it out until the end!

1. Think of three people that would benefit from this Book, and send them a referral link! You will get paid for anyone who sign-ups.

2. If you enjoyed the Book, please consider writing us a review. It really helps to spread the word and get this information out... remember more Bitcoin adoption is also good for you ;) I wish you all success, happiness, health and incredible gains.

Blockchain Masterclass for Businesses and Corporations

Welcome to the Blockchain Masterclass for Businesses and Corporations, where you will acquire the tools to build the blockchain strategy for your enterprise.

By the end of the Book, you will be able to recognize where and how blockchain and smart contracts can be applied within the corporate world. And you will confidently take strategic actions about the technology within your company.

Please note that the Book does not teach you how to code, nor does it offer specific cryptocurrency investment advice. However, Blockchain Fundamentals is still a valuable asset to both investors and programmers. Obtaining a sober and analytic introduction to key concepts of blockchain is the decisive step to succeed in investing and solution-building.

I look forward to boosting your blockchain journey!

Introduction

Hi and welcome to Bitcoin 101, an introductory Book on Bitcoin block chain and the future of money. Allow me to quickly introduce myself. I have over five years experience investing and researching in the cryptocurrency space. I've been interested in this space since 2016 and since that time I've made it my mission to educate my family and friends on this revolutionary new technology. I work with a business called Satstreet, we're Canada's fastest-growing digital asset exchange.

We help high net worth individuals and ultra high net worth individuals get exposure to Bitcoin and cryptocurrency. I also own and am the co-founder of a business called Crypto Weekly. We connect people to businesses and investors in the cryptocurrency space. We also have a weekly newsletter that provides the top stories on everything in crypto and gets delivered directly to your inbox every Monday morning. So I highly recommend you check that out. OK, what will you learn in this Book? First, we start slow with bitcoin and block chain basics. These are understanding the fundamentals, the terminology and the difference between Bitcoin, Blockchain and other cryptocurrencies.

From there, we move on to the Bitcoin fundamentals, these eight characteristics that make Bitcoin so impressive. Moving on, we get into why Bitcoin is so important, not just from a technology perspective, but also from a macroeconomic lens. When we look at the global monetary and fiscal policy, next, we talk about where Bitcoin is headed in terms of price and in terms of adoption. We also make some price predictions as to where we think Bitcoin will go in the future.

From there, we move into the path to mass adoption, how we're going to get to a global adoption. We're currently only at one percent global adoption. So we discuss the three constituencies that need to adopt Bitcoin enabled in order for it to get to that global mass adoption. Moving on, we get to the point of the Book where I know most of you guys are going to be interested in how to buy and store your cryptocurrency. And finally, we finish with a look to the future of what a block chain based future might look like, not only for Bitcoin, but for some of the other amazing projects that are building in the cryptocurrency space. But before we get into that, a little disclaimer.

I'm not a financial advisor, so please do not take any of this as financial advice. I also highly recommend that you do your own research before investing not only in any crypto asset, but in any period. You need to fully understand what you're getting yourself into before you put any money at stake. Second, this market is very volatile, so don't invest anything you're not willing to lose. Next, investing without a strategy is no better than gambling. So when you're going to enter a market, understand the price points that you want to get in it and understand what your target prices are to get out, anything else is no better than gambling. I'm not a Bitcoin maximalist.

I think there are many amazing projects being built in space. But for beginners, it's important to first understand the fundamentals of Bitcoin before diving in and taking the red pill on any of those other more risky assets. A lot of this chapter is based on my opinion, but in many cases my opinion is based on years of research. So I try my best to show my work wherever possible and to provide links for you to do your own research after the Book is complete. Most of the charts in this Book are based on U.S. dollar values, and that's done for two reasons. One, because U.S. dollar data is very prevalent, and two, because the U.S. dollar is currently our world reserve currency. And so it's important to look at things and U.S. dollar figures because it's compatible with the rest of the world.

Now, I don't claim to know everything. I don't claim to be the foremost authority in this space. But I do know I have years of experience, and I would love to do anything that I can to pass that on to you and your family so you can provide financial prosperity for your family moving forward. Now, my motto for life is nothing good in life is worth having unless it's shared. And this is part of the ethos behind this Book. I wanted to share my knowledge on Bitcoin and block chain because I think it is fundamentally a technology for good and I think it is a bastion for free speech, for free will and for the democracy of power around the world. And so I'm so excited to share this Book. But before we get started, I wanted to play a little game. This is called If I had invested a hundred dollars in 2009, where would it be today?

Now we take a look at some of the returns of some of the biggest companies in the world, Amazon, Apple, Visa, Microsoft. Now, if you look at Apple, if you had invested a hundred dollars in 2009, a 24 X return seems pretty amazing... until you look at it alongside Bitcoin. Now, mind you, this was taken in 2019, so the prices are vastly different from there. But if you were to invest in Bitcoin a hundred dollars in 2009, just one decade later, that would be worth 9.2 million dollars and today probably over 20 million dollars.

So we can see that this is a market of scale. This is one of the highest returning assets of all time. And through this Book, I'll show you why that is why that's set to continue and some of the features that we can look forward to in the future if we build the future on the block chain. So with that, thank you for listening to this introduction. I cannot wait to share the rest of the Book with you. This is Bitcoin 101.

Bitcoin & Blockchain Basics

This chapter of the Book is called Bitcoin and block chain basics, let's dive in now first, let's just get an understanding of terminology. There are a lot of different terms that get thrown around in the cryptocurrency industry. And first, let's just set the level with a basic understanding of their definitions. Cryptocurrency, what is it? A cryptocurrency is a digital currency in which transactions are verified and maintained by a decentralized system using cryptography rather than a centralized authority. So you can think about this as, you know, a system of transactions that are verified and maintained, decentralized and using math as opposed to a centralized third party like a bank or a credit card company or an institution.

Now, there are many different types of crypto currencies. So what I've done is I bucket them into three major types. Cryptocurrency is for payment. So these are truly currencies. There are crypto currencies that are securities. So think about those like a tokenized portion of ownership over a certain asset or even a certain stock, like a business. The last use case is for utility. And so this type of cryptocurrency gives you access to a certain network. They allow you to pay for a certain service on a network and are pretty much fundamental to the use of that block chain within the entire cryptocurrency industry. So crypto currencies is a very broad term, but it's kind of a catchall for many of the different projects that are building in the cryptocurrency space. Now, Bitcoin is very different.

Bitcoin is the first ever cryptocurrency, and it's the project that introduced the world to the underlying technology of block chain. Bitcoin is a finite currency, so there's only a certain amount of them, 21 million that will ever be produced in the world. And it allows you to send funds directly, peer to peer, without any centralized third parties in between. Like I said, credit card companies or bank banks, it is a truly global currency and it allows you to transact directly with anybody around the world, which is a major breakthrough.

Now, Bitcoin transactions are recorded on a decentralized network of computers from around the world, and they're secured using cryptography. So it's extremely difficult to hack and it's very secure for sending payments around the world. Now, many people think Bitcoin and block chain chain are the same thing, but block chain, also known as distributed ledger technology, is really just the base layer that all of these different crypto currencies are built on top of. Now, a block chain is a system in which a record of cryptocurrency transactions is maintained across several computers that are all linked in a peer to peer network. So, as we said, decentralized across computers and directly peer to peer block chains, eliminate the need for third parties and counterparty trust. So these are massive breakthroughs for global transactions, for foreign exchange and for the future of global commerce. Those are the three definitions and those are all important fundamentals to understand about the cryptocurrency space.

Now, what is the block chain, really, and I mean, what is a good comparison that we can look at in history, kind of similar to what this what this is and really the best comparison to, you know, the invention of the block chain is the invention of the Internet. The Internet was invented in the 1950s as a data transfer protocol, as a way to send information all over the world. And what that did was it created a massive explosion of information. We could send info now, you know, across the globe with the snap of a finger. But really, the problem with sending information, like, for example, a picture online is if I send a picture, I can still have the copy of a picture and you can have that same copy so it gets duplicated.

Now, that's easy if we're just sharing information. But what about sharing or spending cash? If I send you ten dollars, I shouldn't be able to have that same ten dollars in my account. So it introduced this problem called the double spending problem. How do we ensure that if I send you money, I can't still have that money in my bank account? So what happened was when the Internet was developed, we had to build these layers of security on top of this baseline protocol that was really just for information sharing. It wasn't necessarily built for value sharing. So we built these different layers on top and we created what we call Internet 1.0, which is static information being sent in Internet 2.0, which evolved to being able to communicate and send messages and receive messages online.

Now, the Internet that we have today, as much as we think it's decentralized, it's really owned by a curfew. It's owned by the likes of Apple, Amazon, Google and Facebook, really. And these major corporations are pretty much the gatekeepers of the modern Internet that we have today. Well, what if we had a better solution? Introducing block chain block chain is not a data transfer protocol. It's a value transfer protocol. So at its base layer, it is secure for sending transactions. In that case, security is built into the fundamental protocol. It doesn't need to be built on top by these large corporations that pretty much run the Internet that we have today. This will bring us the Internet 3.0 or the next generation of the Internet as we know it, and it will be owned by many. It's a decentralized technology, meaning it can be owned by everybody and controlled by everyone and developed by everyone. So there are not going to be centralized authorities that are going to be running this space. It's going to be run by the people in the communities that build in this space.

Now, I love to quote here, too, so block chain is the technology, but Bitcoin is merely the first mainstream manifestation of its potential. So we think about Bitcoin as this major peer to peer transaction layer. But there are so many more technologies and revolutionary industries that are going to be built on this base layer value transfer protocol that we call the block chain. Now, in order to understand what a block chain really is, let's first take a look at what a bank really is. Now, at its core, a bank is just a centralized ledger. It's a trusted third party that we trust to send our money from one party to another to record transactions in one account, out of another account, and to make sure that people have the money that they say they have when we do transactions.

Now, every bank has its own central ledger. And so these banks need to reconcile with each other to make sure that each of them is telling the truth. Each of them is saying they have the money that they say they have and to make sure that transactions are recorded properly. And this is a very time consuming and expensive process in the way that we have it today. What if there was a better solution in reducing the block chain? A block chain instead of a central ledger? Is a decentralized ledger or a distributed ledger technology. Now, with the block chain, we instead of trusting a. Centralized third party to record all of the transactions that happen in our day to day lives. We can replicate all the transactions that happen within the block chain, across every computer that wants to run the protocol. So if everybody has copies of the exact same ledger, we no longer have to trust that a centralized third party has it right or that a centralized third party is going to be a good actor in storing and using our data.

Now, when a transaction is recorded on the block chain, it gets simultaneously recorded across all the computers that are running the algorithm. So if a transaction gets approved and it's truthful, it gets replicated across all the computers. But what if you tried to hack one of those computers and put a fraudulent transaction in? Well, if the transaction is secure or if the transaction is not verified by the rest of the block chain, it won't be added to the block chain. So it's very difficult to hack the block chain because in order to hack in, for example, create a fraudulent transaction, you would need to simultaneously hack over 51 percent of all the computers that are running that algorithm around the world and that it's extremely difficult to do.

Another way of thinking about decentralized ledgers that might be a little bit easier is to think of millions of digital accountants that are all working on balancing the same books. Every one of these accountants is like a little computer that's working extremely hard to validate all the transactions that happen on the block chain. And if you wanted to cheat that system, you would have to simultaneously trick over fifty one percent of all those millions of digital accountants that are working on validating the transaction history. And so that's very difficult to do. And this really brings to bear the true benefits of decentralization, a centralized third party or a centralized corporation where all of our data is housed.

And we think about this as all of the major corporations that we know and love today, Google, Facebook, Amazon, Apple, these all are centralized entities. And all these entities are storing all of our data and all of our value. What makes it so scary is that that's one central point of failure. So hackers know exactly where they want to hack and they buy by hacking one system, they can steal the records of millions or billions of people with a decentralized ledger. The risk is very much mitigated because there's no central point of failure for somebody to steal all the information that happened or all the transactions that happened on the block chain. So that makes it very, very resilient to attack and extremely secure and cryptographically secure far, far into the future.

Definitions: Bitcoin & Blockchain Cryptocurrencies

Definitions Cryptocurrency Cryptocurrency is a broad term used to lump in all digital currencies that are built on distributed ledger technology (aka. blockchain). These currencies are also referred to as "tokens" because they can be used for more than just payment. A token could be used for payments (currency). It could represent ownership in a company or a network (stock ownership or certificates of ownership). It could also grant access to or serve a purpose on a network (utility). There are countless cryptocurrencies and some are better than others, just like there are countless companies and some are better than others.

Bitcoin A Bitcoin is a type of digital currency in which new units of currency are generated by the computational solution of mathematical problems. It has a stable, predictable, and sound monetary policy and operates completely independently of a central bank. Bitcoin was the first-ever cryptocurrency and the idea that introduced the world to Distributed Ledger technology.

Blockchain/Distributed Ledger Technology

While Bitcoin is the first mainstream manifestation of this technology, Blockchain is the real technological breakthrough behind the whole thing. It is a system in which a record of transactions is maintained and verified across several computers that are linked in a peer-to-peer network. It is a system with no central authorities, no trusted third parties, just direct peer-to-peer value transfer.

This technology will not be relegated to financial assets, it will be adopted by almost every industry on earth, and has been speculated to be as large a technological breakthrough as the internet. 6. Internet vs Blockchain The Internet In the 1960s the Advanced Research Programs Agency (ARPA) invented a technology for sending information over large distances to assist with military efforts. That technology grew into what we know today as the internet.

Originally, the internet was built as a Data Transfer Protocol. It was a great way to communicate over large distances. Eventually, it became commonplace when applications like email were built on top of it. The internet created a global information explosion, and today we have access to the summation of almost all human knowledge, in the palm of our hands, with only a few clicks. But while the internet is a great tool for sending information, it is not great at sending value. When you send a picture online, it can be copied millions of times and shared all over the world. This is great for pictures, but not so great for money. This brings into question what is called the Double Spending Problem. If I send a dollar online, how does the recipient make sure I do not still have the same dollar?

We need some way to ensure the dollar cannot be double spent online. Today, we put our trust in third parties such as payment processors and digital banks to ensure that our money is safe and properly accounted for. But since all of these companies were built on the "data transfer protocol" of the internet, all of this infrastructure was built on top of insecure technology. Enter Blockchain Blockchain, on the other hand, was built as a Value Transfer Protocol. This means that at its base layer, the underlying technology that's being used to build the applications of tomorrow, is fundamentally secure. With security built-in, we no longer need to rely on centralized third parties to transfer our funds from point A to point B.

Instead, you can transact directly peer-to-peer with no added intermediaries. When security is built in at the base layer, we can also own and control all of our own data. Instead of allowing internet titans like Google and Facebook to harvest and sell our data, blockchain will enable people to own their own data and share it only with parties they choose. Blockchain as technology will democratize power and create a global system that is owned by all of those who use it. 7. Distributed Ledger Technology The Goal of the blockchain is to create a system where all parties can come to a consensus that a transaction happened, without having to trust any other parties. One of the most common institutions we use today to ensure a transaction happens, is a bank.

To understand how the blockchain works we must first understand what a bank fundamentally is. At its core, a bank is just a centralized ledger. Banks have records of all the different accounts in their system, and they help us keep track of money that goes in one account and out of another. We trust the bank to make a record of those transactions. We also trust the bank to ensure that the people who are paying us actually have the money they say they have. We also trust the bank to convert our currencies and send money overseas. When it comes down to it, we put a lot of trust in banks, but banks also need to trust each other.

Each bank needs to ensure that other banks are being truthful and honest about the funds that they hold. And while all banks have their own ledgers, this means they all need to be reconciled with each other. This is a time consuming and expensive process. Enter Blockchain Now, imagine, instead of a bank or central authority recording all the transactions in a centralized ledger – what if the same ledger was replicated and owned by everyone using the system. If we all have access to the same ledger then everyone can verify transactions and come to a consensus that they are correct.

Instead of trusting a centralized third party to make sure that all sides are acting fairly, the blockchain creates a trustless system where no one has to trust other parties because everyone has a copy of the same ledger.

"The blockchain does one thing: It replaces third-party trust with mathematical proof that something happened." – Adam Draper By creating a global network of distributed ledgers, we can create a world where money can be sent freely peer-to-peer without needing a bank or a payment processor like Visa or Mastercard to facilitate the transaction.

Bitcoin Fundamentals

This part of the Book covers the secret sauce that makes Bitcoin so special. This is Bitcoin fundamentals. Let's dive in. Bitcoin has a lot of very unique characteristics. And each of these characteristics or fundamentals would be game changers for society and technology on their own. But when they're packaged all together, they become far greater than the sum of their parts. So I like to call these the unstoppably eight, these eight characteristics that make Bitcoin so truly revolutionary.

Now, we'll go through them quickly here and then I'll go deeper into each of those chapters as we move on. So decentralization, as we already talked about, being so important to reduce centralized points of failure, trust less reducing the need for counterparty risk, counterparty trust and third parties directly transacting peer to peer. So I can send money from my Bitcoin address to somebody in Africa in a matter of seconds without going through a credit card company or, you know, a financial institution.

Bitcoin is permission less. So anyone around the world can create an address and your account or address can't be frozen or shut down by a centralized authority. Bitcoin is secure, built on block chain and cryptography, and run by math and not by people. It's also nationless. It's not correlated to any country or any political party, any celebrity or any stock market. It's truly an asset class on its own and it's truly global. It can be sent from myself in Canada to somebody in Africa with no foreign exchange fees and without going through third parties or banking systems. And finally, I think the most important characteristic of Bitcoin is that it's finite. There's only ever going to be twenty one million Bitcoin in existence. This can't be understated. It can't be printed a way into existence. Like the the dollar is

We printed trillions of dollars this year. And in the same way that gold is a finite resource, there's only going to be so much gold on Earth. There's only ever going to be so much bitcoin available in circulation. So if you have a fixed supply and the demand for it goes up, obviously the price goes up. And having this fixed supply is what truly gives Bitcoin the characteristics of a digital gold or gold 2.0. Now, for all those Marvel fans, this feels a lot like getting all of the Infinity Stones right, becoming all powerful. Bitcoin is truly an entity that cannot be shut down. It's too big for governments. And essentially, if one government tries to shut it down, there will always be other governments that want to build on the technology and use the technology to further their own society. So shutting down Bitcoin is nearly impossible and it's become this entity that's truly a bastion for freedom and for human rights.

And we'll talk a lot about that later in the Book. But first, let's dive a little bit deeper onto each of Bitcoin's fundamentals. This chapter talks about centralization versus decentralization. Now, the majority of the entities we know today are centralized authorities or centralized companies, institutions, and it has become all too common to hear in the headlines. So-and-so's company got hacked, right? We hear about this all the time. And when this happens, millions upon millions of our records get sent out into cyberspace and stolen by hackers.

Now, tell me if you recognize any of these companies. Twitter was recently hacked. Three hundred and thirty million records or accounts were affected. Zoom was hacked, 500000 passwords were stolen. 57 million accounts were hacked. JPMorgan 70 million records hacked. Target 70 million records hacked. Capital One, 100 million records hacked. Adobe 152 million records, Cannava one hundred and thirty seven million records. eBay one hundred and forty five million records.

Equifax one hundred and forty seven. LinkedIn one hundred and sixty five million records. Microsoft two hundred and fifty million records were stolen by hackers. The Marriott five hundred million records hacked Facebook. Five hundred and forty million records were hacked. Yahoo was hacked in 2013. Three billion records were affected and then again in 2014. Five hundred million records were affected and most recently the one that's making all the headline news, the Russian hack of well, let's just push this forward, the Russian hack of the United States government, all these massive institutions, the NSA, the FBI, Homeland Security, all of our records, all of these United States records, these truly confidential top secret records stolen by the Russian government.

Why? Because they were stored on a centralized database. That was one central point for attack. This is why we can't go on with these centralized, decentralized authorities anymore. The future needs to be built on decentralized applications. And that's where Bitcoin comes in. It's been around since 2009, and has never been hacked. No central point of failure developed on a decentralized grid of computers, confirming and processing transactions that happen on the algorithm by math. And so this is the biggest thing. It's an algorithm. It's an organization, a network that's run by math and not by people. We've seen what happens when these organizations are run by people, millions of effects of records, millions of transactions hacked because we can't trust these parties with our data, nor should we trust them anymore.

Bitcoin is just one example of a company or a currency built on the block chain. But the majority of these new companies that are coming up into developing applications on the block chain are decentralized as well and do not have a central point of failure. They're resilient to attack. And so this is truly why it is so important to build a future of decentralized technology as opposed to centralization. OK, let's talk a little bit about trust less. So let's take a transaction. Bob wants to send money to Paul. If he was to do that today, this is what it would look like. He would send money through Visa, PayPal, maybe Stripe or MasterCard.

Now, this money would get sent kind of through these payment processors to a bank and then the bank account would send money into Paul's account. These are trusted centralized authorities. We trust them to make sure that everybody has the money that they say they are and the money gets sent safely from one party to another. Now, let's look at a trust list environment. If Bob wants to send money to Paul, nothing stands in the way except a network of computers that validate the transaction. So in that case, there are many benefits to this.

To raise security in these networks is built in, right, it's not that you don't need to trust a bank. You can just trust that the network will run as it's supposed to. There's no hidden agendas, right? There's no company that is standing in the middle and taking a fee or taking a percentage off of every transaction you make. There's no incentive for a block chain to extract more value. Banks and credit card companies have a mandate. That mandate is to make money in order to make money. What they do is they stand in between you and the purchaser and they take a percentage of all those purchases, just a small percent, one, two, three, three percent, which doesn't seem like a lot.

But over millions and billions of transactions in a year, these fat cats are getting rich off of the transactions between society. So there's no incentive for a block chain to extract more value from you and then there's no more reconciliation. If everybody has the same ledger, one bank doesn't not need to reconcile their ledger with a credit card company or another bank. Everybody has the same ledger. No more reconciliation, no more wasted time and money. And finally, there are no more trusted third parties. We don't understand how many third parties we have in our life because we've never had the technology to be able to cut them out. And finally, everything is networked, validated, so validated by the computers that are running the algorithm. So extremely secure, extremely trustworthy.

Let's now look a little bit more into the peer to peer side of the network. So does anybody recognize this picture? I'm sure you've built something like this as a kid or seen one of these works. This is called a Rube Goldberg machine in an extremely complex machine that eventually does something extremely simple. And it's my stance that this is our current financial system. If you think about what happens when you, for example, pay with your credit card at a store, let's say you're going to Starbucks and you tap your car to pay for a bit of information, and get sent to a dozen different companies.

Now, all these companies have your payment data and they can sell that data to other third parties that want to monetize it. That data gets stored and saved and logged by these other companies. And then eventually information gets sent back to the bank, gets sent to the merchant's bank, and then the merchant's bank processes the transaction and maybe a week later they get paid. This is absolutely absurd that in twenty twenty this is the world that we live in today. Now, as I just said, I don't think we will realize the amount of middlemen we have in our life until technology grants us the opportunity to really cut them out. So let's take a Bitcoin transaction.

Instead of that massive Rube Goldberg machine that's processing the payments, you have a direct payment one to one with whoever is purchasing your product. Now, the benefits of this are massive. There are far lower fees. And if we're talking about foreign exchange transactions, that savings gets even greater. You can send millions, hundreds of millions of dollars on a block chain network from one address to the next for under ten bucks. There is no other way that we've ever had in human history to be able to transfer that much wealth for that. That inexpensive over price transactions are not only cheaper, they're also faster and by orders of magnitude.

So if you think about a foreign exchange transaction or a transaction overseas, you sometimes need to wait up to two or three weeks for that wire transfer to get through. In the case of a block chain, you're turning those days or weeks into minutes incredibly efficiently for international or global payment systems. Finally, no more middlemen. Right? So there's nobody that's taking a fee from your transaction just standing in the middle and waiting for you to rake up all the value. Now, this sounds great for us in the Western world, but let's take a real world example from somebody in the developing world.

This is Malia and this is her story, right? She is from the Philippines. She came to Canada to be a nanny, to provide for her family, so to provide a stable source of income that she could send back to her family in the Philippines. Now, Mallea gets paid every two weeks. When she gets paid, she goes to Western Union deposits. The funds Western Union then sends those funds to a clearing house. That clearing house sends the foreign exchange via a wire transfer. The wire transfer gets to her family's bank, you know, a week or two later and then her family gets to pick up that money from the bank. Now, if she were to send money via Bitcoin, she would be able to quickly put in a payment address, send exactly how much she wanted and have that money sent to her family in the matter of minutes, maybe an hour.

Now we think about that. We don't really fully understand the benefit of this, because most of us reading this Book are not coming from the Third World. But when transactions are sent overseas and the amount is very small, those transaction fees, those wire transfer fees can cut in 30 to 40 percent of the actual value that you're going to send somebody. By the time it gets to your family, they're only getting 60 percent of what you made, all because that's the only way to do it these days.

Now, providing them a cheaper and faster way to transact with their family allows them so much more buying power and so much more economic freedom because of the work that they're doing overseas. So this is extremely important for the developing world and it's just as important for the developed world. But we don't fully realize all the benefits of it because we're so accustomed to a sound financial system. But the benefits can't be overstated for the developing world. OK, let's look a little bit into security. So Bitcoin has a few different ways of securing the network. The first is through cryptography, really complex math problems that these computers need to solve in order to validate transactions on the network. Now, this process of solving math problems and validating transactions is called mining. And I'm sure a lot of you have heard about Bitcoin mining.

We'll talk a little bit more about what that entails. But essentially, you just need to know that that is the process of a computer running a program to mine very difficult math problems in order to validate the truth of a transaction. So it's secured through cryptography. It's also secured through decentralization. Now, we keep hitting on this point, but it cannot be overstated how important a decentralized future is, a future where the power is distributed not in the hands of a few, but to the hands of the many, to the population that is truly making it an economy run instead of that one or two people in the zero point one percent that want all the power to rule overall. Thirdly, Bitcoin is secure through transparency. All of the transactions that happen on the block chain are recorded in blocks.

Now, we'll talk about this when we talk about mining. But it's fundamental to understand that every transaction from one account to another is validated and recorded on the block chain ledger. So you can always go back in history and see when money transferred from one account to another. Now, accounts are crypto cryptographically secure. So they have a 32 digit hexadecimal string of numbers and letters. So you don't necessarily have your name on it on a Bitcoin address, but you can see when money gets sent from one address to another. So the benefits of all this security, again, are immense.

You own your own data, right? If information is sent on the block chain, there are block chains that are extremely secure that allow you to own your own data instead of sending all that data off to third parties. And transactions are verifiable, time stamped and immutable. Once a block is verified on the block chain, the transactions in that block cannot be changed. They are immutable. They're also timestamped exactly the time that they happen. So they reduce a lot of conflict moving forward. In terms of when a payment happened or in what sequence or what process, something happened.

Finally, the protocol, as we said, is open source so anybody can see the code underlying the network and know that it is not it's not used for individual gain for something like Google. Nobody really knows exactly what the goal was, what Google's algorithm is. They keep that so tightly under wraps because that is their competitive advantage with the block chain. It's all open source. You can see all the code, if you would like, on GitHub. But what this does is it not only allows for extreme transparency, but it also allows a community of members from around the world to make additions to the code as they see fit and as the community sees fit to upgrade it.

So it's a protocol that's run and developed and built by all the people that are used by a lot of the people that are using the community. OK, let's talk about permission less, less so there are many benefits of having a bank account that you can open up on your own, that you don't need preauthorization, you don't need to go to a bank. You can essentially have ownership over your own economic freedom. And this is huge, as I said, for the developing world. So the biggest use case of this is being able to bank the unbanked, those people in the developing world that have never had access to a financial institution, they've never had access to their own bank account, which drastically reduces their economic mobility.

So their ability to move up in society and to accumulate wealth. If you don't have a bank account, where do you put your wealth? And so Bitcoin is allowing the people without a bank account to create their own bank account. It's also unstoppable, right? There's no centralized party that can freeze your account. Now, once again, we living in the Western world are a little bit oblivious to this. But there are many countries in the world that with the snap of a finger, all of your assets, if they're in a local bank account, could be frozen.

All of your assets could be stolen away from you by a corrupt government if they don't agree with your views on a certain subject. So it's important to have not only a bank account that anybody can create, but also a bank account that nobody can shut down. In this case, if everybody has access to the same banking systems. They can make their own account. Nobody can shut down their account and they can send money from their account to any account around the world. It creates a system that at its core is built fundamentally as an antiracist system, as an anti sexist system and as an anti dictatorship system.

Once again, decentralization brings power to the edges. It gives power to the everyday people as opposed to all the power flowing to the top with a large government or a Communist Party, for example, power flows down to the community, to the people that make the world run. And this is extremely liberating not only for the developing world, but for those in the developed world as well. Bitcoin as a global currency, so Bitcoin has a very interesting back story and one that will probably live on in folklore forever.

Bitcoin was invented in 2008 by a pseudonym named Satoshi Nakamoto. Now, to this day, nobody knows exactly who Satoshi Nakamoto is. It could be a man or a woman or a group of people. Nobody truly has any understanding of who Satoshi Nakamoto is or where they came from. Now, the genius of this is that it leads to many benefits. Having an anonymous founder allows not only for the currency to be truly global, but it allows for a global currency, allows for no foreign exchange fees because everybody uses the same currency, no currency conversion, so no fumbling between different currencies, a system that can be used around the world by anyone, and also the ability to ensure that no country has the authority to shut it down.

If we knew Bitcoin came from a certain country, that country might either have a leg up on the rest of the world or they might have more authority to ban it. And if Bitcoin was banned in that country, it might be cascading across other countries. But since nobody knows its exact origin, nobody really has a monopoly on the invention of Bitcoin. Because Bitcoin is so global and decentralized, it's also very uncorrelated to anything that we know. So it's uncorrelated to national governments, as we just mentioned, to political parties, uncorrelated to corporations or stock markets, fiat currencies or even celebrity figures.

Now, celebrity figures, it sounds almost like a last minute throw in. But think about, for example, the company Tesla now knock on wood. But if Elon Musk was to ever pass away, what would happen to the future of Tesla? What would happen to Tesla stock? Most likely it would plummet. Now, in the case of Bitcoin, since nobody knows exactly who is Satoshi Nakamoto is, even when he passes away or she passes away, Bitcoin will continue to live on because nobody because it's not tied to that specific person that created it, it's become an entity on its own that is built and run by the people that use it. OK, finally, let's talk about the big fundamental benefit of Bitcoin, and that is that it is finite. So the total supply of Bitcoin will only ever get to 21 million.

Now, this is the total supply, but the supply that is currently in circulation is roughly eighteen point three, eighteen point five million Bitcoin, depending on when you're reading now, just like gold has a finite supply and there will only ever be a certain amount of gold either above ground or below ground on Earth. The same thing applies to Bitcoin. There will only ever be a certain amount of Bitcoin, either total supply or in circulation. As we continue to mine gold, we also continue to mine Bitcoin into circulation. Now, the interesting thing about Bitcoin is that roughly 20 percent of the entire circulating supply has already been lost.

The private keys of the people who own Bitcoin have been lost. Hard drives have been thrown away with thousands of Bitcoin on them. And these Bitcoins will most likely never come back into circulation. They'll never be transacted again. And so if you have a supply that is not only finite, but is also diminishing because people continue to lose their bitcoin, lose their keys, you have a perfect storm for an asset that holds its value and that actually increases in value over time as the more demand starts to pick up for it. But how can we be sure that there will only ever be twenty one million Bitcoin if we continue to mine all this Bitcoin?

How do we know that there are only twenty one million? And that's where the genius of mining comes in. Now, mining is essentially, as we said, running a computer algorithm that solves very difficult math problems to validate the truth of a transaction. So if I wanted to back in the day in 2009, if you wanted to set up your computer as a mining rig, you literally would need to download the Bitcoin application and start running the Bitcoin algorithm on your computer.

Now, things have changed a little bit and mining has become a heck of a lot more difficult. Three point eight million computers around the world are now mining the Bitcoin algorithm and the computers, the hardware that are mining these algorithms has gotten so sophisticated it can't be done on a simple laptop or desktop computer anymore. There are these specific mining computers that are built only for the sole purpose of hashing, of adding power to the Bitcoin network and transacting and validating transactions. OK, so how are these blocks mined and what really is Bitcoin mining on the bitcoin block chain? Every 10 minutes a new block is mined.

Now you can think about a block as if it was a pool of transactions. And you have this computer that's scooping up a bunch of these transactions, packing them together in a nice block, and then adding that block to the previous block. This happens roughly every 10 minutes on the Bitcoin block chain. You have a bunch of computers that are all competing to be the first one to validate a certain block to. Be the first one to solve this math problem and validate a certain block and add it to the block chain. Now, if you own the lucky computer that wins that block, you get paid a mining reward. That computer gets a reward in Bitcoin and those bitcoins get taken out of the total supply and into the circulating supply. So that is the process of mining bitcoin into circulation.

Now, every 10 minutes, these blocks are added, and with each block, hundreds of transactions are added to the block chain.

And so these transactions are now verified. They're now time stamped and they're now logged on the Bitcoin block. Now, as I said, the computer that wins or solves that problem the quickest gets a mining reward. But what is the mining reward? Well, when Bitcoin was first invented in 2009, the block reward was 50 Bitcoin. So every 10 minutes, a computer was earning 50 Bitcoin. Not every single computer, but the computer that wins the block reward gets 50 Bitcoin.

And then something that was built into that's been built into the code since its inception. But in 2012, something called a having happened for the first time, which means every four years Bitcoin goes through a cycle called a having. Then instead of the block reward being 50 Bitcoin every 10 minutes, the block reward gets cut in half to twenty five Bitcoin every 10 minutes. This happens every four years like clockwork, and it's built into the algorithm and it's built into the price. And we know it to be true. So the first having happened in twenty twenty twelve and from twenty twelve to twenty sixteen the block reward was twenty five bitcoin then from twenty sixteen to early twenty twenty the block reward was twelve point twenty five bitcoin and then in May of twenty twenty the block broadcast got cut in half for a third time to six point twenty five bitcoin.

And the same thing will happen in twenty twenty four and in twenty twenty eight and then in twenty, thirty two and so on. And what happens when you have this diminishing return every four years, the supply being cut in half. You have these step changes right where the supply gets cut in half every new supply gets cut in half every four years and the circulating supply eventually approaches. Twenty one million but never actually gets to twenty one million. It will get very, very close. But as we continue to cut those circulating supplies continually in half, you'll just be mining less and less and less bitcoin every ten minutes. This is truly genius. This is Albert Einstein.

This is The Da Vinci behind Satoshi Nakamoto, creating this algorithm to make a finite resource in the digital world. We've never really had that before. And it is truly what makes Bitcoin so remarkable, because the finite resources are finite, the more demand there is for the resource, the higher the price goes up. The price is really a fundamental feature of the Bitcoin algorithm, not a byproduct. OK, that was a lot of information. But let's do a quick recap. Bitcoin's fundamentals, it is distributed trust less peer to peer permission less secure, location less correlated, sorry, uncorrelated and finite. These are the fundamental eight. And that's what makes Bitcoin unstoppable. We'll see in the next channel. See in the next chapter.

The Unstoppable Eight

As we discussed in the previous chapter, bitcoin is just one of many cryptocurrencies. However, Bitcoin specifically has some characteristics that make it extremely unique. I call these fundamentals, "The Unstoppable Eight." Each of these fundamental characteristics on its own would be massive improvements to the current monetary system that we use today.

However, when you put these characteristics together they create something that is stronger than the sum of its parts. These characteristics together make up a coin nearly unstoppable.

Decentralization A decentralized network has no central points of failure and no ownership or authority figures. The network is owned by nobody, yet operated by everybody. Trustless Bitcoin removes the need for counterparty trust. We now have the ability to trust in a mathematical algorithm, as opposed to having to trust other humans and an agreement.

Social media and fake news has caused our trust to irreparably erode in society. Everyone has an opinion on what is true and what is not. Blockchain is the first time we have ever been able to look at the cryptographic proof of a transaction and know for certain that something happened. The applications of this level of trust are truly inconceivable.

Everything from voting, to supply chains, to identity and health records will be impacted by the blockchain. Peer to Peer

Bitcoin has no intermediaries. Transactions are sent directly from one address to another. It removes the need for banks, payment processors, and trusted third parties. Permissionless The bitcoin network is open and accessible to everyone. There is no need for an application, no one who can tell you your account has been closed, and no need for formal verification. Anyone around the world can open a bitcoin address. Therefore, it is a tool for financial inclusion and a way for the disenfranchised to get access to the new financial system.

Security Bitcoin is built on a cryptographically secure blockchain framework. It is secured through network validation, cryptography, and decentralization. Security is built-in, so we don't need to rely on third parties to keep our assets secure. Global/Nationless Bitcoin is a global currency. There is no foreign-exchange, no wire-transfer fees, and it can be accepted anywhere around the world. This revolutionizes foreign exchange and dramatically increases human mobility.

Uncorrelated Bitcoin was invented by an anonymous founder or founders known by the pseudonym Satoshi Nakamoto. No one knows exactly who invented Bitcoin. For this reason, Bitcoin is not correlated to any country, any political system, stock market, national currency, or celebrity figure. Because the founder is anonymous, the technology has the opportunity to far outlive the person or people who invented it.

Finite Bitcoin is assigned a commodity. There will only ever be a maximum of 21 million Bitcoins. Some of those Bitcoins are not yet released in circulation. Some of those Bitcoins are already lost. We cannot print Bitcoin into existence in the same way we choose to print dollars into existence whenever there is a crisis. Bitcoin's monetary system is fixed, stable, and predictable. These qualities give Bitcoin its value.

Distributed

To reiterate the value of the decentralized network, I have listed a few centralized companies that have been hacked in the past decade. Take a look through some of these companies and see if you recognize any of them.

Hacked International Corporations (Centralized)

Twitter: 330 million records affected – 45 celebrity accounts hacked Zoom: 500,000 passwords stolen Uber: 57 million records compromised

JP Morgan Chase: 70 million records

Target: 70 million records affected

Capital One: 100 million records

Adobe: 152 Million records affected

Canva: 137 million records affected

eBay: 145 million records affected

Equifax: 147 million records affected

LinkedIn: 165 million records affected

Microsoft: 250 million records affected

MySpace: 360 million records affected

Marriott: 500 million records affected

Facebook: 540 million records affected

Yahoo: 2013 – 3B records affected / 2014 – 500M records affected

US Government: (Homeland Security, NSA, FBI, Treasury) Full extent unknown. I left a link below to a website called https://informationisbeautiful.net[1]. Here you can find a visual rechapter of all the major data breaches from multinational corporations over the past decade.

No longer should we be trusting our information to centralized companies, time and time again has betrayed our trust. Visualization of Major Data Breaches: https://www.informationisbeautiful.net/visualizations/ worlds-biggest-data-breaches-hacks/

Bitcoin (Decentralized)

Bitcoin has never been hacked and it's almost 13-year history. It has no central point of failure, it is resilient to attack, and it is owned by no one, yet run by many. It is a system run by mass, not people. However, bitcoin is just the first application of this technology.

We are now building decentralized applications on the Blockchain. This will enable a new generation of decentralized organizations that can do all the same things as the companies on this list. However decentralized applications allow you to own your own data and to profit off your own information.

---

1. https://informationisbeautiful.net/

Here is a link to a website that allows you to explore all the new applications that are being built on the blockchain.

Many of these applications will overtake the centralized applications we know and love today. The blockchain is simply a better faster stronger technology than the legacy internet that these companies were built on.

DappRadar: https://dappradar.com/

Peer-to-Peer

Who remembers building these as a kid? Today's current financial system reminds me a lot of a Rube Goldberg machine... You tap a card somewhere to pay, a bitstream of information gets sent to a dozen computers, and three days later the transaction is settled and someone gets paid. Not to mention, along the way dozens of companies get access to that payment information without paying you a cent for it.

We give this data away as if it was worthless, yet last year data surpassed oil as the most valuable commodity on earth. Why is it that we give so much of this away and see none of the rewards? Enter Bitcoin What Bitcoin promises is that we can cut out the middleman. I firmly believe that we won't realize how many middlemen we have in our lives until technology grants us the opportunity to cut them out. Bitcoin offers direct peer to peer transactions, and this has enormous global ramifications.

Imagine you are a nanny and you have traveled to Canada for work in order to send funds back to your family in the Philippines. In our current system, you would have to go to a Western Union, who would send your money to a clearinghouse to convert your currency, who would then send your money through a SWIFT transfer, who would then send your money to a foreign bank who would then have your money roughly 3 weeks later.

With Bitcoin, that same nanny can send funds to her family without any middleman taking a cut off her funds or adding time to the transaction. Typically, bitcoin transactions are settled within half an hour. This is a massive step-change in the way we do international exchange.

Trustless

Trustlessness is a quality of the blockchain network meaning that you do not need to trust any centralized party to ensure the transaction is made. Instead of putting your trust in an organization or in a government or in humans, you can trust the math.

Whenever we make a transaction, we trust a credit card company or bank, to ensure that the money gets from point A to point B in a reasonable amount of time. You also have to trust that the person who pays you, has enough money in the bank account for the transaction. We trust banks and credit card companies to create security around one fundamental problem with the Internet. This problem is called the double-spending problem.

Permissionless

Bitcoin is a permissionless network. You do not need a license, a bank account, formal verification or pre-approval to open up a Bitcoin account. For the first time in human history, everyone in the world has access to economic empowerment in the form of a bitcoin address. This allows them to participate in the economic system and store their economic wealth.

Banking the Unbanked Because anyone can open a bank account, no one has the authority to shut down your account. Unlike bank accounts that can be frozen or shut down by the local government, Bitcoin accounts cannot be frozen or turned off, they are truly unstoppable. Currently, in America, African Americans are less likely than whites to be approved for new bank accounts and to be accepted for a mortgage.

The permissionless nature of the Bitcoin network is the great equalizer. Now everyone is on the same playing field. Because every account is treated equally in the "eyes of the ledger" regardless of race, religion, geography, sex, or otherwise. Blockchain technology is fundamentally anti-racist and anti-sexist. Anti-Authoritarian Moreover, Bitcoin is Anti-dictator. Because the money supply is fair and predictable, no one is in control of the creation of new money. Therefore no one has the power to manipulate the money supply. Distribution of power reduces the likelihood of tyrannical leaders rising to power.

This fundamental of Bitcoin cannot be overstated!

Secure

Security With blockchain, security is priority number one. Bitcoin derives security from three pillars of its design. Cryptography The bitcoin blockchain uses state-of-the-art cryptography to keep information safe. Transactions and addresses are fully encrypted.

A bitcoin address consists of a 32 digit alphanumeric code. Decentralization Decentralization is another key pillar of bitcoin security. A distributed network makes it resilient to attack and almost impossible to shut down. Transparency The bitcoin blockchain is fully open-sourced, meaning anyone can see the bitcoin code. This is important because bug fixes and improvements can be crowdsourced by anyone using the software.

Transparency is also important in understanding the flow of money. You can track where a bitcoin was spent when it was produced, in which wallets it has been sent to. All transactions on the blockchain are time-stamped, verified, and immutable meaning they cannot be changed.

Lisk Academy – Is the Blockchain Safe

I have links to chapters from a YouTube channel called Lisk Academy. In this chapter, they discuss if the blockchain is safe. 15. Global / Nationless One of the most interesting concepts tied to Bitcoin is its origin story. This is because no one knows exactly who created Bitcoin.

Satoshi Nakamoto In 2008, at the peak of the financial crisis, the Bitcoin whitepaper was mysteriously released on the internet by a pseudonym named Satoshi Nakamoto. The whitepaper started as an idea, but quickly gathered steam in the cryptography community as an interesting project.

Over the Book of the next decade, the network has evolved into a global asset class, with over $200 billion dollars in market cap, and over 3.8 million computers running the Bitcoin algorithm, and still, no one knows who Satoshi Nakamoto actually is!

The anonymous nature of this project actually gives it some amazing properties: Not correlated government, the stock market, or political parties No country can shut it down No national borders No foreign exchange Link to Bitcoin Whitepaper: https://bitcoin.org/bitcoin.pdf

Uncorrelated

Because Bitcoin is so global and decentralized, it is also very uncorrelated to different markets and economies around the world. Another way of saying this is that the performance of Bitcoin does not mirror the performance of any other asset classes around the world over large periods of time. Because it is truly Global, it does not correlate to:

National: No national party can run, shut down, or affect the money supply Political Parties: It does not advance the ideals of any specific political party Corporations: It is not tied to the performance of any global corporation (unless the corporation chooses to hold its treasury reserve in Bitcoin)

Stock Markets: Any correlations that have been proposed between Bitcoin and stock markets have been short-lived. Bitcoin has outperformed every stock market in existence today since its inception. Fiat Currencies: It is not tied to fiscal or monetary systems of any countries, nor to the amount of money printed by any national government.

Celebrity Figures: It is not tied to the actions or antics of its inventor, because no one knows who Satoshi Nakamoto is. It is also not susceptible to devaluing if the founder passes away. This enables Bitcoin to stand the test of time and live on far after Satoshi passes away.

Portfolio Risk Uncorrelated assets are helpful in reducing risk within a balanced portfolio. Therefore, even though Bitcoin can still be thought of as a volatile asset, it has a place in the portfolio of the biggest hedge funds and investment managers in the world.

Finite

Probably the most important feature to take away from Bitcoin is that it has a finite total supply. There will only ever be a maximum of 21 Million Bitcoin in existence. As we will learn in the next chapter of the Book, the scarcity of a resource is one of the crucial factors to its utility as money.

As of today, we have mined over 18.3 million Bitcoin in circulation, and what's crazy is that more than 20% of all Bitcoin in circulation is already LOST! Just like gold sunk to the bottom of the sea, these Bitcoins have been lost because their owners have misplaced or lost their private keys.

Gold vs Bitcoin The reason gold has value is that there is only a finite amount of gold on earth. We can mine it out of the ground, but we cannot simply print more of it whenever we feel like it. Mining gold takes a lot of work, and the only reason we continue to do it is because there is an economic incentive to keep doing so. Bitcoin is very similar. There is only a finite amount of Bitcoin, we cannot print more of it. We can mine Bitcoin by running a sophisticated computer algorithm, but it takes a lot of work (electricity). Miners continue to mine Bitcoin because there is an economic incentive to do so.

In the next chapter, we will learn more about Mining.

Finite Continued: Mining Mining

If you have ever heard of bitcoin before, you have probably heard of the term mining or mining bitcoin. What this means mining is the act of the computer solving difficult math problems in order to validate the truth of a transaction. Every computer that runs the bitcoin algorithm is constantly performing complex computational work to verify that a transaction took place.

Proof-of-Work The Bitcoin blockchain runs on a proof-of-work consensus algorithm. This means, in order to validate transactions, computers must perform complex computational work in order to show proof that a transaction occurred. Each computer that is running the Bitcoin algorithm is working towards solving the complex math problem in each block. The computer that solves the math problem first gets a reward for the block that it solved. This is called a block reward. Roughly every 10 minutes a new block is solved (mined) on the Bitcoin blockchain.

The Bitcoin Halving Roughly every four years, the block reward on the Bitcoin blockchain gets cut in half. From the Genesis block in 2009 to the middle of 2012 the reward was 50 Bitcoin. That means every 10 minutes 50 new Bitcoins were mined in the circulation. In 2012 the block reward was cut in half to 25 bitcoins.

Meaning every 10 minutes 25 bitcoins were mined into circulation. From 2016 to Q1 2020 the block reward was 12.5

bitcoin. And just recently on April 22, there was a third having and now the block reward is 6.25 Bitcoin. The function of cutting the block reward in half was programmed into the Bitcoin algorithm since inception. This predictability is one of Bitcoins' most important features, but we will discuss that later. Simply Explained – Mining This chapter goes more in-depth on how Proof-of-Work mining works on the Bitcoin Blockchain.

Why We Need Bitcoin

This chapter is called Why Is Bitcoin so Important? In order to figure this out, we first need to take a look back in history and really learn the difference between currency and money. Now, I'm sorry to break it to you, but the paper dollars we use today are not necessarily money. They're actually currency. And there's a major difference. So currency is a generally accepted medium of exchange within a group of people. So a society, a community and currencies have changed greatly over time.

In fact, ancient China and Europe used to use seashells as currency. Later on in China, Mongolia, they use things like tea leaves, compressed tea leaves in BRICS as currency. In fact, in a remote island in the Pacific, in the Pacific Ocean called Yapp, they actually used massive bricks of limestone carved into circles or wheels as money or as currency. Now, today, the majority of the world uses pieces of paper as currency and currency has some of the same characteristics as money. But there's one major difference.

Money is a generally accepted medium of exchange as well, but it is also a store of value over long periods of time. So for many years, gold was that store of value gold. And the reason gold was a store of value is because it's finite. There's only a certain amount of gold on earth and it couldn't be just printed into existence. So Gold did a very good job of holding its value over time because there was only a scarce amount of that gold. And this has worked for over 5000 years until the invention of Bitcoin. Now Bitcoin is widely referred to as Gold 2.0 because it has many of the same characteristics as gold. And let's figure out what those are. So as we said, let's take a look at currency first.

Currency needs to hit a few different checkboxes in order to be kind of generally accepted as a medium of exchange or in a society. So the first is that it's a medium of exchange rate. It's generally accepted amongst the population as a way to trade for things that they need. Second, it needs to be a unit of account. So you need to know how much of this currency you need to pay for a certain good or service. Third, it needs to be portable. So you need to be able to bring it from place to place. You need to be able to exchange hands.

Different people need to be able to own it and transfer this currency in order for it to be generally accepted. It needs to be durable. So at least in the short term, it needs to be able to weather storms and hold its value, at least in the short term. It needs to be divisible. You need to be able to make change and you need to be able to pay fractions of, you know, for fractions of a good or service. You need to be able to make change with that currency. And finally, it needs to be fungible. And what fungible means is if I give you one dollar, you don't necessarily have to give me back that exact same dollar. You can give me any other dollar that's in circulation.

You can also give me four quarters. And that is the same value as one dollar. So it means it's exchangeable and accepted in different ways. Now, money needs to have all of those same characteristics as well, except the seventh one is that it needs to have it needs to be a store of value. It needs to be scarce.

So you can't just keep printing it into existence and making more of this money. That's what gives it that store of value. And the reason gold and bitcoin have that is because there's a finite amount. Now, let's now take a look at gold versus Bitcoin.

Well, Bitcoin is now becoming more of a medium of exchange. Gold, I would say, still checks that box more in today's day and age. But as we continue to get to mass adoption, we will see Bitcoin becoming a much better medium of exchange than gold. And it's easier to transact. It's easier to pay. Bitcoin is actually a better unit of account than. Old it is divisible into one hundred million satoshi, which are the equivalent to a cent to the dollar, so you can break a Bitcoin down into a hundred million different pieces. That also makes it extremely divisible. It's even more portable than gold.

Imagine trying to take a flight with, you know, one hundred million dollars worth of gold. That would be a heavy suitcase. Imagine now trying to take a flight with one single ledger or hardware wallet that stored a hundred million dollars worth of Bitcoin. A lot easier to travel, a lot easier to bring from place to place, and therefore a lot more portable. Bitcoin is very durable, but gold is also extremely durable. These are two characteristics that are very well matched. The reason Bitcoin is so durable is that it only needs one computer to be running the Bitcoin mining algorithm in order for the ledger to stay intact.

Currently we have over three point eight million computers running that ledger. And the more computers that run it, the more secure the network becomes. So as that number of computers that are mining, the Bitcoin algorithm continues to grow, Bitcoin becomes more and more durable. Bitcoin, as I said, is extremely divisible, far more so than gold, which gives you a higher money value. And it is also a lot more fungible, right? It can be exchanged for payments. It can be used for cross-border transactions that can be used in many different ways and accepted now even more so than even last year by millions of different vendors.

PayPal, for example, just opened up Bitcoin payments to one hundred million merchants around the world. Square is doing the same thing with their cash shop. And so it's becoming a lot more fungible and a lot more a lot easier to use as a transactional value. So for those reasons, Bitcoin truly is Gold 2.0. And on top of that, the finite scarcity of Bitcoin is known, whereas the scarcity of gold is not fully known, it's not fully realized. So these are very, very important concepts to understand the difference between true money and the currency that we use today. And currency does not stand the test of time.

Every single government currency that has ever been printed in human history has eventually gone to zero. And the reason is because governments continue to print, because they continue to spend more than they earn and the currency eventually gets inflated away. Now, let's take a look at known history and what brought us to the point that we're at today. So this is the history of world monetary systems and bear with me because this is a little bit of a longer chapter. But it is truly important to understand how precarious the situation we're actually in right now. So for much of the late eighteen hundreds and into 1914, much of the world was on a classical gold standard.

This meant governments would print their own money and that money would essentially be a receipt for gold. It would be a claim check on gold. Gold was held in the banks of those countries and then the dollars were used as claim checks. Whenever you needed to get your gold, you would just slap your money, your government currency down on the bank and they would give you your gold back. Now, in the case of the United States, the exchange value of twenty dollars was equal to one gold coin and there was a one to one ratio. So for all the gold coins that were in the bank, there was an equal amount of dollars that were flowing around in circulation.

Now, the reason they use dollars is because it's a lot easier to carry around a stack of paper than it is to carry around a bag of gold coins. So this made it a lot easier for societies to transact. And then 1913 rolled around and the Federal Reserve was invented, the Federal Reserve was invented, but also at the same time as the First World War. So the First World War was going on and we didn't have enough money to pay for it. So what the United States government did was they started printing more dollars than they had gold coins and reserves.

And as a result of that, what they did was they caught on to this gold exchange standard first they said, you know what, we're we're stopping gold redemption, right? So you're no longer going to be able to go to the bank with your dollars and receive your true money, receive your gold instead. You're just going to have to use those dollars and that's going to be the end of discussion. What they did was they moved on to this gold standard in order, the gold exchange standard in order to pay for this war, so they printed more money than they had gold in reserves.

And now instead of having a direct one to one ratio of dollars in circulation to gold and reserves, we had what was called a 40 percent reserve ratio of gold. So for every 50 dollars that were in circulation, there was only one gold coin, even though they were still supposed to hold the same value as 20 dollars equal to a gold coin. This is very troubling because this is really the first time the United States government started to lie to the American people and print more money than they actually had. And this was in order to pay for the war. So this standard lasted for roughly 30 years and until the Second World War rolled around. So Hitler took power in 1933. And by 1936, he was waging war against most of Europe.

And when this happened, the countries of Europe needed to pay for goods and supplies to pay for that war. And who did they turn to? They turn to the United States. So all the while, while this war is being waged in Europe, these European countries are sending their gold to the United States and the United States is sending goods and services back over to these countries to pay for the war. So what happened by the end of the war was that the United States had two thirds of the world's gold reserves. Now the rest of the world had about a third, but there was almost no gold left in Europe because they needed it to pay for the war. And so by 1944, global governments came around and they met in Bretton Woods, New Hampshire, and created what they called the Bretton Woods system.

They needed to create such a fundamentally new role for currency, because if citizens of Europe wanted to exchange their dollars for their euro currencies for gold, the banks in Europe didn't have enough gold to supply them. And so there would be a run on the bank. So the whole world economic system could collapse if this run on the bank persisted in Europe. So they got together in Bretton Woods, all these world superpowers, and they said we need a new system. The United States really became a global superpower because of all this gold that was transferred into their country over the Second World War.

And we need to have a way of pegging our dollars or our currencies still to the gold, even though the United States is in control of most of the world's gold. So what did they do? They took all of their global currencies and they pegged them to the dollar. And then that dollar remained pegged to gold. So we still had a system that was pegged to something pegged to gold, but it was a trickle down effect from all of these currencies that could then be transacted into U.S. dollars. And those U.S. dollars could be then returned for gold. So this worked for quite a few years until really nineteen fifty nine when France was the first country to say, hey, who's really checking the United States gold reserves?

We don't know if they're just continuing to print money because they have so much gold in reserve. So how can we trust the United States that they're going to be good actors in this situation? And as it turns out, France was right, the United States, because they had so many gold reserves, they just started printing money like no tomorrow because their dollar essentially became like gold for the rest of the world. And what France realized is that nobody was holding them accountable.

Nobody was checking on the gold reserves that were actually in circulation and how much currency they had in ratio to that gold. So as it turns out, by 1971, the United States had printed 12 times more dollars than they had in gold reserves. They were using this, you know, this system was created for them in order to make them rich. And they did. They got rich. Off of it, until a bunch of these countries started repatriating their gold, France was the first. But, you know, from 1959 to 1971, most of the countries started to repatriate their gold. They said we don't trust the system anymore.

We want our gold back in our own country. So we have a kind of sovereign control over it. And what happened in 1971, Richard Nixon had to take the dollar off the gold standard, because if all of these countries continue to repatriate their gold, they wouldn't have enough gold to pay for all that, to pay all the countries back because they had printed so much money. So what happened was Nixon in 1971 had to come off the gold standard. And from 1971 until today, we've been on a dollar standard. So what that means is we have these currencies that are pegged to the dollar and then we have the dollar that's pegged to nothing. So the United States has really removed any peg to real money that this currency currently has and how this didn't start another World War I has no idea. But what's happened is that we've now created a currency system that's not pegged to anything that can be printed into infinity and that will continue to be inflated away for as long as these governments continue to print.

Now, as we get to 2020, we see how much of a problem this is as governments are printing trillions and trillions of dollars on an annual basis in order to pay for covid-19. So this is a massive problem that we really haven't seen the full effect of yet. And I'm sure it's coming soon. Now, as I said, we have dollars that are backed by nothing. But on top of that, we're lending out dollars that don't even exist. We call it credit. Banks are loaning out money that's not even in circulation and they call it credit. So you need to pay back those dollars plus interest to the bank because they're lending out money that's not in existence.

And currently we have a global debt to GDP ratio of over three hundred and twenty two percent, meaning the debt that we have on a current current scale is over three times more gross domestic product than we make in a year as a globe. This is a truly, truly scary place to be in. Now, we can see right here from this chart why the dollar is not money and it's not money because it doesn't hold its purchasing power. This is a graph from 1913 when the Federal Reserve was invented to twenty thirteen, but it continues to chapter after that. And so from that time, the United States dollar lost ninety eight point five percent of its purchasing power. This is not a store of value. This is a currency, so we need to get that.

We need to first understand that in order to understand why Bitcoin is so important. So cryptocurrency is a powerful concept that can overturn almost any government. And the reason it can do that is because it's sovereign. It can't be printed into existence. It's finite. So as we look back in history, in the current chapters that we just kind of reviewed, we can see that there's a new global monetary system that emerges roughly every 40 years.

The classical gold standard was from between 30 and 40 years. The gold exchange standard was 30 years. Bretton Woods was twenty eight. And now we've gotten to this dollar standard that seems to have overstayed its welcome. We've gotten over 50 years on this dollar standard with this money that is pegged, sorry, with this currency that is pegged to nothing. How long can we continue to print? How long can this printing engine continue to run before the wheels fall off? We don't know that. But what we do know is that over and over again in history, the pendulum of this kind of currency has always swung from quality money to quantity currency.

And the reason it does that is because governments and people are greedy. They print more than they consume. They overpromise and then they print to pay for those promises and they debase the currency that they have because there's always an incentive for a politician to over promise and then pay for those promises by debasing the currency. That's always been the pattern throughout history. And this pendulum will eventually swing back to quality money. And I think we've hit this far side of the pendulum now when we see printing going into the trillions of dollars each year.

The United States government printed twenty five percent of the total US dollars in circulation this year. This law of diminishing returns will eventually take effect where you can no longer print money to stimulate your economy because that money isn't doing anything. This is why in Germany, when they went through a hyperinflation, they needed to go to the banks with wheelbarrows full of cash because that cash was not was not worth anything. This is back in history. But let's take a second to understand GDP, right? Gross domestic product. This is a gross domestic product. So really, your gross domestic product of a country is just the velocity of money. So how many times that money is changing hands? At times the money supply. So how much money is there in circulation times?

How fast is money moving around the economy now in a strong economy, in a real growth economy, that you increase the velocity of money because you want many people exchanging value and you want all of that money to be changing hands so people have freedom to spend on things that they want. That is a true growing economy. That's a really good economy. Now, on the other hand, you can have artificial growth, you can have artificial growth in GDP, and that's just by increasing the currency supply. So even though that currency isn't doing a lot of things, it's not moving around. It's not touching many hands.

The velocity of money is slow. You can still, on paper, say you're increasing GDP just by increasing the currency supply. And look where we are today. These are graphs from the Federal Reserve, the Federal Reserve, economic data. And we can see this is the velocity of money. So the M1 money supply, how fast is it moving now? Ever since the financial crisis, two thousand eight, we have been falling off a cliff. The velocity of money has been slowing so fast and now we get to twenty twenty with covid and it's hit a wall. It's falling to zero. People aren't spending money anymore. And on top of that, technology is very deflationary as well.

People don't spend as much money on things because technology makes everything cheaper, faster and stronger. So you don't need to spend as much to get the same amount of marginal goods. This is very scary. We're having not only a currency that's being devalued, but also a currency that's not moving around the economy. And so this lifeblood of our economy is starting to slow. You can think about it like human organs, right? Or the human body. Money is a lot like blood. Blood needs to circulate around the system in order to keep everything healthy. If that blood circulation stops, the person dies. So we're in a very scary place where we're velocity of money is going to zero.

And at the same time, we are printing trillions and trillions of dollars. So there's this kind of offsetting effect that allows us to say that our economy is growing at one or two percent. It allows us to say on paper that, you know, these things look good not to scare people, but this is where we are today. We have a currency that's being diluted and the velocity of money that's slowing. And there needs to be a safe haven. You need to have a life raft. You need to have a way out. Bitcoin can be that life raft. Thank you. I know this was a long chapter, but I hope you enjoyed it. And I look forward to seeing you in the next one.

Currency vs Money

Currency has been many things over the years. Limestone was used on a remote island called Yap in the Pacific Ocean. Shells were used as currency in ancient China and Europe. Later Tea Leaves were used as currency in China, Mongolia, and Parts of Russia. Now we use pieces of Paper as money all over the world. All these currencies share some fundamental qualities, however, they all lack one thing that confirms they are not true money. Definitions Currency - A generally accepted medium of exchange within a group of people. Money - A generally accepted medium of exchange, as well as a store of value over time.

Currency and Money share many of the same characteristics. However, money requires one quality that currency does not. There is a reason why currencies have changed and adapted over time, but true money has stayed the same for thousands of years. Currency must be:

Medium of Exchange - A way for people to transact.

Unit of Account - Can keep track of prices and how much is owed.

Portable - Can move with people, and be traded amongst a community.

Durable - Can withstand wear and tear.

Divisible - Ability to make change.

Fungible - Must be interchangeable (if I give you a dollar bill, you can give me a different dollar bill and they are worth the same) Money must be:

Medium of Exchange - A way for people to transact.

Unit of Account - Can keep track of prices and how much is owed.

Portable - Can move with people, and be traded amongst a community.

Durable - Can withstand wear and tear.

Divisible - Ability to make change.

Fungible - Must be interchangeable (if I give you a dollar bill, you can give me a different dollar bill and they are worth the same)

Finite - Must be a scarce commodity, and able to hold its purchasing power over large periods of time.

The History Of Money

Timeline of the Recent History of Money 1873: (Classical Gold Standard) Most of the developed world was on the Classical Gold Standard – Governments print their own money, each dollar is a receipt for one gold coin stored in the treasury 1913: (Federal Reserve Was Invented) 1914 (World War I) : Governments stop Gold Redemption Rights so they can print more dollars than there are gold coins to back them (Fractional Reserve Lending) Between World Wars we moved to the Gold Exchange Standard – $50 were only backed by $20 of gold (40% Reserve Ratio) 1933: (Hitler Takes Power) 1936: (World War 2) - America Benefits American Troops did not touch down in Europe until 1942. For 6 years the United States was making the supplies to fund WW2 and all the European countries were paying in Gold.

So at the end of the war, there was little gold left in Europe, but lots of US Dollars 1944: (The Bretton Woods System) After the war: The United States owned the vast majority of the global gold reserves. 2/3 = US 1/3 = Rest of World 0 = Europe (but Europe was flooded with USD Loans) If this current system continued, European banks would not be able to pay out gold for citizens that wished to hold it.

A global bank run could have occurred and the entire world monetary system would have collapsed. World Superpowers met in Bretton Woods, New Hampshire to come up with a new world monetary system called the Bretton Woods System 1959 – 1971: (United States Abuses Power) France Realizes the US can print endless currency and get into endless debt – starts repatriating their gold Other countries start repatriating gold The US Lost over 50% of its gold reserves 1971: (Dollar Standard) The US had printed 12x more dollars than there was gold Essentially there was a worldwide bank run (with the US being the bank) Nixon Forced to take the US off the Gold Standard and move to a new Dollar Standard Dollars are now backed by absolutely NOTHING and can be printed to infinity 2020: We now lend out dollars that we don't have in the bank and call it CREDIT.

USD Purchasing Power

Using our definition of Currency vs Money from Lecture 20, we can clearly and unequivocally see that the United States Dollar is not money, instead, it is currency. To understand this, we need not look any further than the purchasing power of the USD over time.

Since the Federal Reserve was invented in 1913, the US dollar has lost over 98.5% of its purchasing power (a figure now closer to 99%). Every time the government prints new dollars, they steal purchasing power away from the dollars that were already in circulation. The overprinting of money can lead to higher prices for goods, or even hyperinflation in extreme cases.

COVID Printing The problem is, with economies shutting down due to COVID, the only way governments around the world were able to keep their economies afloat was by printing excessive amounts of money. This is unsustainable in the long term, and will inevitably lead to hyperinflation and increased economic disparity.

Effective Federal Funds Rate (Interest Rate): https://fred.stlouisfed.org/series/EFFR M1 Money Supply (Money Printing): https://fred.stlouisfed.org/series/M1 US Unemployment Rate: https://fred.stlouisfed.org/series/UNRATE Learn From History Every fiat (government printed) currency ever created in human history has eventually gone to ZERO.

This is because politicians always have an incentive to overpromise and to "borrow from the future" by printing more money in order to pay for their outsized promises. Moreover, no government has an incentive to pay back the debt of the last government, so the can keeps getting kicked to the next administration until the whole system unravels. We can learn from history... sound money leads to lasting prosperity.

The History of Monetary Systems

Changing Monetary Systems The Dollar Standard is now almost 50 years old. The average age of a person on earth is less than 30 years old. This means an overwhelming percentage of the global population has never experienced any other monetary system other than the Dollar Standard, with the USD as the global reserve currency.

This can create the illusion that we have always been this way, and that things will never change. However, when we look back at history. We can see that changes in monetary systems are actually more common than you may think. Overstaying our Welcome Over the past 150 years, we have had a new monetary system roughly every 40 years. However, the Dollar Standard has managed to remain for nearly 50 years, which means we might be due for a change.

In fact, in October of 2020, the Managing Director of the IMF made an announcement that the world is in need of a "New Bretton Woods moment". The excessive amounts of printing and national debt that have arisen from the response to COVID-19, have left the world in a very precarious position. If a new standard is not created, the entire global economy runs the risk of breaking under the weight of all of our global debt.

Over and over in the thousands of years of human history, we have seen nations rise and fall based on the principles of sound money. When an economy has sound money, the people can prosper. When governments overprint, it leads to inflation, inequality, and ruin.

The pendulum of history over and over again has swung from quality money to quantity currency and back again. The invention of Bitcoin gives us the ability to finally swing the pendulum back in the direction of quality money.

The New World Order One thing that has been made clear as a result of this announcement, is that many developed countries are now working on building their own Central Bank Digital Currencies (CBDC's). This will allow central banks to have direct access to inject funding into the bank accounts of individuals around the country. These CDBC's will be built on some variation of blockchain technology and will create far more monetary and fiscal policy levers for central banks to pull in times of crisis.

GDP 101

In order to fully grasp how acutely we need a new monetary system, we can look at our calculation of Gross Domestic Product. GDP is, "the total dollar value of all goods and services produced in a country over a year. It is sometimes referred to as "the size of the economy" and includes all consumption, government spending, private investments and the foreign balance of trade (FBOT)."

This may seem like a complicated figure, but we can simplify it by saying the following: GDP = Velocity of Currency (how fast currency moves around and economy) x Currency Supply (how much currency is in circulation) Because one half of the equation accounts for the amount of money* (in this case currency) in circulation, governments have the ability to artificially inflate GDP just by printing more money.

There are two ways to increase GDP: 1.REAL GROWTH: You increase the velocity of money, meaning more money changes hands and more value is created. 2.ARTIFICIAL GROWTH: Inflate the money supply so goods cost more, and therefore more money changes hands. What we have seen over the past decade falls very much in the camp of artificial growth. The Velocity of currency has fallen ever since the financial crisis of 2008, and has fallen off a cliff ever since COVID. All the while, the currency supply has been growing at a breakneck pace ever since the financial crisis and has been going parabolic ever since COVID. These trajectories are not sustainable.

Why We Can't Just Keep Printing The problem with printing more currency is that every time you do it, the marginal benefit of the new funds diminishes. Said another way, with all the quantitative easing measures that the United States has gone through since 2008, it feels like we have shot seven rounds of an eight-round pistol.

Once the velocity of currency goes to zero, no amount of new currency in circulation can improve the economy. Article: USA Today - US is `printing' money to help save the economy from the COVID-19 crisis, but some wonder how far it can go: https://www.usatoday.com/in-depth/money/2020/05/12/coronavirushow-u-s-printing-dollars-save-economy-during-crisis-fed/3038117001/

Cryptocurrencies from A-Z The First Steps in Crypto

Do you want to learn the Fundamentals of Cryptocurrencies from A to Z?

Do you want to learn how to buy/sell cryptocurrencies?

Do you want to learn how to make a passive income through cryptocurrencies?

Do you want to learn the most important terms used in the crypto industry?

Do you want to learn how to use the Metamask wallet?

Do you want to learn the most important ways to make money from cryptocurrencies?

Do you want to learn about market correction and when is it good to buy your favorite projects?

Do you want to learn the Fundamentals of Cryptocurrencies from 0 without spending a lot of time reading dozens of tutorials?

If you answered "Yes" to any of the above questions, you should stop here. This is the right Book for you!

This Book is easy to understand and is designed in explanatory video format to convey basic information about Cryptocurrencies in a way that makes everything clear and simple. You will receive detailed explanations with examples.

The Book begins by defining blockchain technology and cryptocurrencies, the most widely used terms in the industry, and ends with the introduction of the Metamask wallet and the chapter of the most important sources of information.

Stop thinking, enroll up today and learn the Fundamentals of Cryptocurrencies from A to Z!

Introduction and Book overview

So. Hi guys. And welcome to this complete practical Book on crypto training. So first of all I'd like to thank you all for joining my chapter. That's really awesome guys and thanks for all the support. So when we were joining this chapter I guess you joined because you probably saw all the profits that were made by cryptocurrency. So if you think of the example of the Bitcoin, the Bitcoin when it was launched on the market was lent less than once then and right now it works more than fifty thousand dollars US.

So Of course it goes from 10000 to 20000. Well it moves a lot. But the main thing is that you would make a lot of profits if you invested $1000 in 2010. Right now you will have millions and millions of dollars. About 50 million. I'm not mistaken. So yeah the object of this chapter if we take a quick look at it it will help you understand how cryptocurrency works. So you will see how it works. While it gains value or doesn't gain value, what's the difference between cryptocurrency and other currencies and the difference between cryptocurrency and stocks?

Also you will see the basics of crypto currency trading well as you can see it's a basic chapter. It's for people who are just starting to use cryptocurrency. So in this chapter you will learn how to buy equipment to sell crypto and how to trade groups to what are the different trading platforms. So you will be able to trade by yourself for that on those reading platforms. You will understand the difference between investing and trading.

How to invest in cryptocurrency and how to treat cryptocurrency. So yes you will basically see all this in this chapter and what's cool is it's a chapter that goes fast. So it's not a 5-6 hour chapter.

I'm talking straight to a point. So we got to go point by point and I can guarantee you that at the end of the chapter you will be able to go by yourself and the crypto currency exchange and be able to treat the crypto that you like treated work invest in it work however you want it can be a daytrader encrypted currency you can invest in cryptocurrency. As I said, it's your trading style. You've got to love it. So let's see the plus win. So first of all right now we're in the interim so I'm just presenting the glass.

The next guest will understand what cryptocurrency is and the major cryptocurrency theory is. So we're going to talk about the major cryptocurrency. There's And I'm going to explain what this group sees in general. After that we don't see how to buy major cryptocurrency with money. So that's in the next chapter. So for trading crypto you have to put money to buy some script first and then you get a trade crippled crypto. So for example you're going to treat the BTC DDH. So Bitcoin exchange rate bitcoin for 3M for example because there are not a lot of exchanges that you.

Well there are almost no exchanges and to get to where you are going , treat your money like it was dollar or euro where the Japanese yen is for cryptocurrency directly. So it's really crippled crypto. After that we had to learn how to build a cryptocurrency wallet. So it's in the chapter 3 so under explaining what a wallop and how to build one point the it were doing and while it's true that I'm going to start our trading trading we're going to learn what are the major artery exchanges and how they work. So you're going to have live news on how they work and you will be able to create an account on three of those exchanges going to show you three principal exchanges will be able to try them with demo accounts. And the one that you prefer you can go live on it.

So real money and buying the coins were two that you wanted to start trading with. After that I'm going to shoot some trading strategies. So we're going to talk about how cryptocurrency trading works. So as a day trader I'm trading for X so I'm going to show you some trading strategies with cryptocurrency. It's a bit different but the bases are almost the same. Well for my strategy. Many other strategies have completely different bases. But from my personal strategies Well the bases are not quite different.

After that we're going to learn how to invest in cryptocurrency projects so when you're treating your day tree truly can swim. But when you're investing you put your money in you don't touch it. You put it on hold and you're waiting until the capital grows by itself. For example when you buy bonds. Well if you buy a used bond you're going to put your money in it and you've got to wait for it to grow.

So it's the same thing with cryptocurrency when you're. But you can buy a bit quaint and traded daily where incredibly well you can buy Bitcoin and just hold it. So for a long time they brought it on a long time and that's it with all this you will be able to treat your Crypto prints. So yes I think once again thank you guys for doing chapter and see you in the next chapter. We're going to understand what's at cryptocurrency.

Cryptocurrency And What Are The Major Pairs

So once you get help guys. And welcome to your second chapter of our crypto currency complete her practical Book. I'm sorry. So the subject of this set in glass will be understanding what cryptocurrency is and what the major beers are. So a cryptocurrency is different but at the same time it looks like a normal currency. And that's what we're going to see in this glass. So let's start from the beginning. So the main question that we can ask right now is what is equipped to currency.

So first of all crypto currency is a digital asset. So it's a bit on the side. It's a bit different from a normal currency because it's just digital and crypto currency is only on the Internet and is 100 percent digital. There is no physical good attached to the digital true true to the digital currency. So and a normal currency or fiat currency that's the term of the normal currency has a physical has something physical attached to it. So we can have physical money but not with a digital asset.

For example, for a big coin or a light coin or curium, think cryptocurrency uses a decentralized system. What does it mean? It means that there is no bank or no central institutions that control the currency itself. Let's take an example of the dollar. Well the U.S. dollar you have the Central Bank of America that backs this dollar you have the government that backs this dollar that makes it legit. And in this way people will trust in the dollar and will use it as an exchange to exchange goods. But for cryptocurrency there is nothing that backs the crypto itself like let's take Iran dumb crypto currency.

Let's talk about, for example, the dash coin. The desiccant is a popular cryptocurrency but there is no real entity that backs this coin like there is no central bank or not. There is no government that backs this point. That's the difference. And so cryptocurrency works by blotching. So what is blotching? Well it's a Tibble. Digital ledger of economic transactions that can be programmed to record not just financial transactions but virtually everything of value. So that's the definition really in the book 10 revolution that is brought by Danny. ALEX SCOTT I suggest this book is very interesting to read if you want to know a bit more about blotching technology.

So as I said it cryptocurrency has no central bank behind it and use that blotching technology to be secure and to guarantee security to the users so users are going well they use Blumstein technology and that what makes them secure that what brings us to our second point of understanding the difference between well understanding what's fiat currency and what's cryptocurrency. So I explained what cryptocurrency is right now. What's the FIDE currency fiat currency is a currency that is regulated by a central government.

Like I said, for example the government of the USA regulates the US dollar and the same thing for example for the Japanese yen. Well the government of Japan regulates the Japanese yen. What about me? What's that that is making the value of the currency legit. Because if there were no government behind it that means that the currency will just not be something legit.

What is the same between the five during and cryptocurrency is that with both of them you can buy goods but with five joints you can buy goods everywhere like for example you go in a shop or in anywhere and you can buy things but with a cryptocurrency can just buy things in certain places because not everyone tests in cryptocurrency.

So not everyone will want to use it as Exchange. So at first Bitcoin was used only on the dark web to buy stuff. But right now it can be used in some places in particular to buy things like for example some shops accept to be paid in bitcoins. I also read that right now there are some people who sell their homes in bitcoins and that's a bit funny because the Bitcoin fluctuates a lot. So you can lose a lot of money but at the same time make a lot of money if you have the Bitcoin at the right moment. So that's the only thing that makes the fiat currency look like a cryptocurrency is that with all of those differences you can buy something.

But in the West it's completely different because one of the currencies is backed by a government but the other one is backed by nothing and just crashes in one second. So if the currency just crashes Well you cannot sue no one because there is no government that backs it. Our last point is what are the major currencies. So as I said in the intro Well it's very hard to trade the U.S. dollar for example for trading platforms with four different crypto currencies. What does it mean? It means that you have to buy major crypto currencies and with those major crypto currencies by other crypto currencies. So when I'm talking about major crypto currencies I'm talking about the bitcoin ethereum bubble.

And yet the one that said those are the biggest crypto currencies right now. And if you want to trade on trading platforms as I said, well it's going to be cryptocurrency. Of course there are some drilling platforms that accept to trade dollars for cryptocurrency or yen for cryptocurrency but those platforms are Fergies brokers for example. Booker Well it's possible to trade major crypto currencies with dollars but the fees are very high. When you make those kinds of trades. So let's talk about the major crypto currencies.

First of all you have Bitcoin. This is the first cryptocurrency that was created. It was released in 2009 and the way it is now where it's around thousand dollars U.S. I think after that you have D.M. that comes in second place and Rippon that comes in third place also backed by big companies. And after that dash Of course you have a lot of other crypto currencies that are for the crypto currencies that are very liquid right now. Well those are the four first but there are some other crypto currencies like for example Monday money or ethereum chapteric or a light point they're also liquid. But those four are the most liquid at the moment.

So I suggest you when you start trading trade just the most liquid crypto currencies because it's going to be easier for you to sell them and buy them and the fees will be less than if you buy it random cryptocurrency that no one knows because when you're trading cryptocurrency the fees that you're going to pay for a cryptocurrency that has a little volume of trades will be very high compared to a cryptocurrency that is very very liquid. So right now we said what's the difference between a fiat currency and the cryptocurrency.

You should understand what cryptocurrency is in how it works. Well you will not really need to know how it works to trade in the group documents you weren't just in to know what the cryptocurrency and that yeah. So that concludes our chapter and in the next chapter we are going to enter the key to creating a world and we got to see how to buy major crypto currencies. So see you in the next chapter, Skase.

Buying Major Cryptocurrencies With Money

So once again. Hello guys. And welcome to your third Book of your complete practical Book on crypto training. So in this third chapter I learned how to bite major crypto currencies with real money. This way you will be able to start the cryptocurrency world. So first of all why do you have to buy two currencies with money or Fiat. That's money that is disturbed by the government. For example U.S. dollars or you. Well it's a good way for you. First of all it's a good idea for you to start in crypto currencies by buying cryptocurrency.

The second thing and the most important thing is that when you are trading cryptocurrency it's better for you to create crypto to treat unspecialized crypto currency trading platforms. Because as I said before, if you want to trade the U.S. dollar for cryptocurrency with margin Well you have to work with us there. It's not all the brokers, all the cryptocurrency brokers that offer it. When they offer it well the fees are very very high.

And normally this kind of thing is offered by for example as you can trade cryptocurrency with some for exhibitors and you can trade with U.S. dollars for example. But it's going to cost a lot. So the best way to start for you is to buy cryptocurrency. So for example you buy a bitcoin or ETM you can buy or it 3M. Well those are the major ones with the U.S. dollar. And after that you can go on any trading platform and you can trade your crypto for other crypto currencies.

For example if you want to read ethereum for some less popular cryptocurrency is going to cost you a bit less than if you're trading one dollar for those crypto currencies and it works the same way when you want to sell your cryptocurrency when you sell a cryptocurrency there is not that much popular. You have to sell it for another trip to Guernsey for example. I don't know if you even have cryptocurrency. You will have to sell it and they sell it for us dollars because you cannot sell this cryptocurrency for us. Delicate no one will buy it. And if the butcher is buying it back. Well it's going to cost you a really really big amount. So what are the main ways for you to buy cryptocurrency? So first of all you have cryptocurrency investing platforms.

When I'm talking about investing in platforms I'm sorry I'm talking about platforms like Coinbase. So on Coinbase it's a platform where you can buy your cryptocurrency. What's cool with it is that you can buy it instantly if you're paying with a credit card. You can't buy it on steam , you can use paypal, you can use wire transfer. They accept a lot of painting methods. If you're there, I think about a lot of countries but not other countries. So you have to be careful. So yeah it's a good way to start for you the fees are not that high also. So once again that's really cool because it's not going to cost us. And after that it's very easy to transfer your bitcoins from the base wallet to your proper wallet.

We're going to see how to make wallets in our next chapter. For now we're just going to concentrate on how to invest in cryptocurrency. So they already offer you a wallop on their website that you can use to stock your cryptocurrency. And after that you transfer it to your wallet. It's very secure also. That's what 's cool. The next thing is cryptocurrency trading platforms. So just then when you're trading cryptocurrency you can go on some platforms and you can already buy your bitcoins with U.S. dollars. So some trading platforms don't accept that you have to come with bitcoins and bitcoins. But in some trading platforms you can buy your bitcoin or your TVM with US dollars and then treat it. So that's another way for you to buy cryptocurrency.

And what's cool also is that it's not margin trading. So you have it here. It's yours like let me give you an example. When you're trading with for example routers It's a contract on difference. So you buy Bitcoins by you but you don't own the Bitcoins you're going to own the defense on the profit or the loss. So for example the Bitcoin is $1000. It goes down to $500. Well you don't and the bitcoin you own the last 500 if it goes up $500. Well you own the profit on the euro the Bitcoin itself but what's cool with those trading platforms is that you've got to be kidding. But there is no margin trading, that's the only thing you treat Ali.

The Crypto that you have so you can not treat on margins. Well some platforms, well some cryptocurrency platforms offer that margin trading but once again the fee is going to be a little higher because they're taking more risk. The best way for you to bedquilt currency is in the Bitcoin terminal. That's easy. Very interesting because you can pay with cash. So those terminals I don't know if they're world wide. You have to look where they're at. Exactly. And with that in the United States there are a lot of Bitcoin terminals and in Canada there are some of them also there are some in Europe.

I don't know if it is in Asia. So you have to look if there are some bitcoin terminals in your region in Europe where you're living. So this way you can buy your bitcoins cash. The problem with Bitcoin terminals is that the fees are very high. For example where I live the fees are about 10 percent so if I'm buying Bitcoins world's going to be 10 percent more than the actual price and if I want to sell one well it's going to be 10 percent less than I will have for my bitcoin. So if you want to have your money cash Well you can do it with it going it seems so if you buy for example your bitcoin two years are going right now you want the cash you don't care about being nice.

Well you can do it with Bitcoin terminals. So terminals don't really suggest to you I suggest you point base. That's a very good way to start in cryptocurrency trading. So you will have your own crypto. And after that you want to transfer it to your wallet. It's very easy and. So let's make a summary. So three ways to buy cryptocurrency is first of all investing platforms: Quinby Coinbase segment killing platforms. It's once again it's not operating platforms that offer you the possibility to bite your cryptocurrency with cash. So some of them will ask you to come with your own cryptocurrency.

So you really need to have big bitcoins in this way you just use one base and the last one bitcoin terminal. It will give you your money in cash. So yes it's cool to have the cash but the fees are very high. So if you're selling Bitcoin Well these are high. If you're buying Bitcoin it's going to be much higher than it really costs. So thank you for reading this chapter guys and see you in the next one. We're going to learn how to build a cryptocurrency wallet and understand what cryptocurrency is.

What Is A Crypto Currency Wallet

So hell yes. And once again welcome to this new chapter of our complete practical Book on playing. So first of all congratulations you're over the edge, you're in the fourth chapter and in this chapter we're going to see what a cryptocurrency wallet is. So now you should all really understand what parenting is and how to buy major cryptocurrency with your money. Right now it's time for you to build up your first wallet and then to see in the scores. What is it and how do we build it up? So let's start first of all what's the utility of it.

Cryptocurrency Well if we're understanding this what to understand what is equipped to convince you of all that. Well it's what we can see as a bank account but instead of storing your cryptocurrency you are going to store your public and private key which in turn helps you send and receive money. In other words it means that you are not storing the crypto itself because the crypto doesn't physically exist. So you're just storing the key. And with this keep Well you are able to make transactions in the future. So let's see how it works. A cryptocurrency transaction. So this way you will be able to understand a bit better why it's storing only the private and the public. So let's do this. So let's take this example.

Imagine you want to send money to someone so you will need it in the cryptocurrency. Will you send money? You need the public key of the other person and you need your private key to send money. So you just enter your private key in the public key or the other person and you click on send. So the first block will be created, that's in other words the transaction itself will be created and the transaction will be sent everywhere on the network. But don't worry, everything is secure. So it's sent everywhere and then it just has to be approved. That takes some time. So it depends on how much you are paying.

Well it's going to take more or less time. Their fees are always less than the bank fees. But the majority of time you choose how much fees you have to pay. In some cases it can be no fees or it can be fixed fees. But it depends. But in the majority of times the well right personal use. Well I was choosing the fees that I was paying. So what's happening next? After that your transaction is going to be stored on the block chain. So what this means is that the transactions are recorded in history on the block chain so other transactions are there.

Well once again it's very anonymous and secure because your name will never appear, you just have the code. The code that you have generated will appear but your name will never be anywhere. And at the end well you the person to whom you have sent money will receive her money. So as you can see it looks a bit complicated but when you're making the transaction the only thing that you have to do is enter your credit. You enter the public and you have the person you want to send money to inject and sell.

And as I said sometimes well maybe there are some fees which are in crypto currencies but the majority of time you are choosing how much fees you want to pay depending on how much easier paying well the transaction will take more or less time. That's the only thing. So right now you understand what a wallet is and how equipped currency transactions work. And what's also the utility for one. Let's see all the kinds of wallets that exist because there is not only one type of wallet there are a lot of them. So the first step is that desktop wallet. So what does it mean a desktop Well it is an application that you can install on your desktop. And with this application you will be able to store your crypto currency. So it's like when you're installing your bank account application for example on your computer.

Well you will be able to look at your bank account balance on this down application is the same thing with cryptocurrency it's an application that you put on your computer and you are able to view your balance on them. There are online wallet's those types. For example, let's talk about Coinbase. Well we'll talk about it in our last chapter but Coinbase is a crypto currency exchange that helps you make transactions with real money. But at the same time it helps you bond cryptocurrency with real money. But at the same time it can sturgeons that it can store descriptive for you on its system.

So Coinbase is the type of online wallet because Quimby's you will not just buy cryptocurrency we're selling it. You can also store so you can transfer cryptocurrency from another wallet to your client base wallet. In other words you can see a wallet like a bank. It's a form of bank because you can just transfer money from one wallet to another wallet. After that we have the mobile wallets. I like desktop wallets more just on your phone. So once again it's an application that you're going to install on your mobile and you will be able to look at your account balance.

So it will be stored on this wallet. So there's some wallets that are working on the desktop as my desktop wallet. And at the same time online. So those three are a bit too secure. Well while in our security industry I personally find them a little bit less secure because they are very vulnerable to hacks and outright attacks online attacks. After that we have the hardware wallet. Well what does it mean?

First of all it's an offline wallet. So this type of wallet can be key for example. So you're just storing all your cryptocurrency on it. For example, we're on the hard drive. But this hard drive stays off of the computer. So you can just put it in your room somewhere and it's stored. So what's cool with that is that there is no one who can attack it by computer. But once again you have to be careful not to lose it because if you lose it. Well guess what. You just put all your cryptocurrency the same thing with the paper. This type of white light is a bit special because you're going to take your crypto currency and transfer it in your code on paper.

Yes it's possible. You don't but we're not gonna see an editorial about how to do it. But just for you to be informed that you can do it you can transfer your cryptocurrency on a paper. And as I said for a while it will not store the cryptocurrency itself. It's just storing your private and public key. So you just transfer your keys on the paper and after that the only thing that you have to do is enter your entry in your key on another wall and to just transfer money from your paper wallet to your online wallet or desktop wallet. So the two there are for me the more secure. So the way I work I never let too much of my cryptocurrency on one of those wallets.

The majority of them stay on a hard drive for any paper. I prefer a hard drive because I don't like paper. So I'm starting the majority of my things on the hard drive. What was the key and I only put small amounts of crypto on desktop online were mobile applications mobile wallets. I'm sorry. So I use the cryptocurrency that is on those. Well it's trading. And the one on the hard drive. It's just we can say it's for investing purposes. I'm just holding it to sell it later. But for the moment I don't want to be I don't want it to be hacked. So I'm just not using it. I left it on the beach. So that's a guess.

Right now you understand what cryptocurrency is, while how it works and how a cryptocurrency transaction works. And the next chapter will build up your first wallet. And when you get to see two that exist, they are very simple to use. And one of them you will see are desktop wallets so you will be able to use them. So see you guys in the next chapter to build up your first wallet.

Building Your First Cryptocurrency Wallet

So once again. Hello yes and welcome to your chapter of our complete practical Book on crypto trading. So congratulations. You know right now by Major cryptocurrency is what all acts of violence that exist and what it is. So the main objective of this chapter will be for you to build up your first Wallack. So as I said if you already made it, Quimby's account already has an online wallet. But what I suggest you do to have is a desktop wallet.

So I personally use a desktop wallet. I prefer this to an online wallet. I think it's more secure. But once again it's your choice. So we're going to see two very very interesting stocks today. The first one is a wallet and the second one will always be. So I'm going to show this chapter out and stop all of those wallets. So how to install it in your wallet and what you can do with it in your wallet and ours and what you can do with us. So install it in your wallet. It's not that hard. You just go on Google and you write down if you don't want it you will be there.

The first one ethereum project so the word you just click on it and you will be on the main page of curium just there you click on download. So when you click on download. Let's do it. So you just click on open with certain ZIP file management default. So when you open it, it's going to create a file. It's just there you just click on the file, click on extract and put it on your desktop. So I'm going to do it with you. So you're choosing a desktop. You click on OK. When all this is done you will have a small folder just their name. When I was 8:32. So we just click on it and you scroll down and you will have a small application there that is named ethereum wallet. So you just click on it and it's going to open by itself. So what I don't like with ethereum wallets, even though they're very interesting Wolf is that they take a lot of time to download.

So yeah you need to have a good network. It's very interesting. While it. So we're not going to open it. So when you're there you just choose if you want to go on the main network or the network. I suggest you go on with this network just to learn how it works. Once again this wall is not installed on my computer so I'm just going to show you the basics. So you could use that test that works. It will tell you to choose a password. So I don't know. So you choose the password. Let's say our best word will be to click next. So it will create an account.

After that what's going to happen. Well it's going to download blocks. So as I said the swap is not downloaded on my computer. So we will. I'm not going to show you how it works but it's not that hard. You just look almost the same way as it is if you want to transfer money. But what's cool with the ethereum wallet is that when you're going on your ethereum wallet Well you can create yourself smart contracts. What does that mean? It means if one day you start programming in solidity Well you will be able to create yourself your smart contract.

For example if you want to make a call if you want to, even if you want to create your own cryptocurrency that you need and you tell them all this. So this way you will be able to create an ethereum based cryptocurrency that is going to be your own cryptocurrency and you will be able to treat it how you want so that what's cool with ethereum will. So let's see our signal. Well so the second word about which one I will start and do this is once again it's a very secure wallet. Very interesting. And it's also a desktop wallet. So I hope the exhaust is just right down it. So this wallet and it's going to be the first one once again. So is money plugging assets.

You click on it so it will be this page that will be opened. You just click on download once again you download it for example. What's cool is that it takes no time to download. So you can download it in seconds. So when the download is very well you open up the app and that's where you will be. So as you can see what's cool is that you have a lot of cryptocurrency. So it's a multi wallet quip. It's a multi multi crypto Wally. I'm sorry. So what does it mean? It means that you can store a lot of types of wallet in it so you can receive payments in a lot of types of wallets for example Bitcoins Bitcoins cash Bitcoin go there it hear your voice. So as you can see there are a lot of crypto currencies that are accepted by others.

So how it works. That's your portfolio where you see how much money and get how much money in U.S. dollars you have of each cryptocurrency after you get your wallet. So you can send for example cash and gold coins or a receipt. So if you receive money, if you want to receive money well you just get a receipt and you ask a person to send you money and the person will just send you the money. Once again if you want to send what you just click on send and the amount you want to send. And let's say Yes. Point one hundred million. Let's say he wanted to put one and send that address. I don't know. We have an address but right there. Are you going to write the address?

Do you want to send it? That's the price in U.S. dollars so it's going to be credited on your account. And as I told you in the last chapter there are some fees. So that's the fees that are asked. As you can see it's 64. So the transaction will cost you 2064 or this amount on Bitcoin. It's going to be charged in bitcoins. What's cool about this is that you also have an exchange so you can exchange your cryptocurrency for any other cryptocurrency. So let's say you have I don't know you have for example Oxx where we can exchange them to you through them.

Once again you have Bitcoins you have let's say one bitcoin Well you can exchange it to 10 million. So the transaction will cost you the difference between this and this. So it's about $200. But once again you are able to make those exchanges. After that we have the backup set to protect a bit more in your wallet so you can transfer your crypto in the backup. And yes so as you can see it's very very easy to use. You have one for your wallet. You just need to keep it there. It's very easy to use. As I said you have a lot of cryptocurrency zealots that are supported by exotics and they always add some new ones. They work only with the most popular cryptocurrency So that's once again a good thing.

Cryptos are very liquid so it's very easy to exchange them. And yet as you can see a lot of crypto is very easy to use. So you can exchange it, you can transfer it. So for example you want to transfer your money you want to transfer you want to transfer your money in cash. Well you can do it with this wallet but you can take the money in bitcoins for example that you have there transferred to your bay. To your credit base account and just conformant it in cash. So it's possible also you can that's what's cool with this while it is.

You can see any kind of crypt to transform it into bitcoins. And then just transfer your bitcoins to your account and with your Quimby's account transfer the money in cash so you can use cash money to transform your money in bitcoins up here because it spreads a lot of crypto currencies. It just takes months. And the point once again is that it is a very very secure wallet. So there is no problem with it. If you see the reviews on the Internet you're going to see it's very very secure and very friendly to use. And. So once again thank you guys for reading. And that see you in the next glass where we start our trading turn and learn about some trading platforms.

Conclusion

So well yes. And one call is welcome to your Less best or a complete practical Book on crypto training. So let me congratulate you. You just completed one other chapter on the unit. So the objective of this last chapter is to make a quick summary would you. Yes. So this way you will not forget anything when the chapter is done. So let's start at the beginning of the Book. I bumped into just a small Book of review. We saw what is a cryptic Drancy so that it's just like in normal currency.

Well it's different from democracy but it is used for the same things so technically it should be used to buy and sell stuff. But it's more used for investing purposes. Also if top of the major appears right now we talk about the ethereum Bitcoin and Ripl dash and all the major cryptocurrency that exists. After that we saw how to buy crypto currencies. Well Major cryptocurrency with real money. In other words with fiat money. So we talked a lot about old code Coinbase in this Book. So I'll explain to you how you can bite currency, how you can sell your own, how you can sell descript to currency and also what's cool with these.

As I mentioned to you, Coinbase is already a wallet and online wallet and storage of your cryptocurrency after that. That brings us to our next chapter: what is cryptocurrency. Right there will talk about what the key difference is that it doesn't really stop stock cryptocurrency stocks, just the private key and the public key. And then after that we saw the tax filing that exists and I explained to you how to build up two different worlds. So the first one that we've talked about is exhorter. So it's a desktop wallet.

What's good is that it's easy to use. It's very friendly to use. It's easy to install and you can convert your cryptocurrency in any cryptocurrency you get what we're talking about only the major beer and also it's very easy to convert your cryptocurrency to any major beer cryptocurrency. After that we'll talk about ethereum wallets. So once again it's a very interesting wallet because you can create your own smart contract on it and you can call in solidity on it. That's the coding program. And for that we've started our trading team. So that's where I explained to you the different exchange that exists.

We've talked about two for beginners. There are bear tracks better next and correct than the one that I suggested to you because in tracking what we can make some margin trading. That's something that is very interesting. But once again you have to practice before starting merger trade and margin. After that we sell some more advanced trading platforms. I'm talking here about etre Delta where you can buy all the crypto currencies that are made from deuterium because in this group in this exchange if mean is the base currency. So what's cool with that is that you can buy all the cryptocurrency that have been made by 3M because as I mentioned you with the German wallet you can build your own cryptocurrency.

And the last one is for Iggs brokers. With those brokers you were able to treat your currency with fiat money, a thing that you can't do with just cryptocurrency Brooker's you can just read cryptical crypto. But with four legs, it's possible. After that we saw some trading strategies. So we'll talk about two different trading strategies. Once again you have to practice before in real world trading. So before using real money I suggest you practice on a different account. What school is that? Well you can't use a demo account with cryptocurrency Brooker's but I suggest you can just download an account with any for example. I suggest that you have a tree but you can if you have any other preference Well it's up to you.

You can open an account with any book that you want and you will see how it works the same way. Just in for example just you know treat fiat money for cryptocurrency and would normally would with cryptocurrency Butros you are going to treat Crypto. After that we saw the difference between trading and investing. That's where it is for short term purposes. And the best thing is for long long work, very long term investment purposes and how to spot great crypto currency projects so you can spot the grid during the project and why you should if you want to invest in it. Well you should invest in it. So we've talked about what you have to look at in it.

I hope to be able to invest in that. So yes. So finally guys once again thanks a lot. First, it's growing for this Book. Thanks for your support and I hope you liked it. If you like it. Well like you. If you don't like it, just don't be an incumbent. Why? And don't forget to read the Book also. So thank you guys for reading. And see you maybe in another of my chapters.

Also by SHAKRUDDIN KHAN

The Smart Way To Personal Finance Success
Goal Setting 101 Achieve More Goals Than Ever! Faster!
Blockchain Masterclass for Businesses and Corporations